A Month of Sundays

Villa Life in the South of France

Ira & Barbara Spector

Arius Publications

Arius Publications
121 Edelen Avenue
Los Gatos, CA 95030

ariuspub@hotmail.com

Cover from an original oil painting by H. Amala,
St-Tropez, France

Chapter art by Barbara Spector

Library of Congress Control Number: 2003093203

ISBN 0-9660-3691-3

First Edition
Third Printing

Printed in the United States of America by:
Patsons Media Group
Sunnyvale, California
408.732.0911
www.patsons.com

From the Authors

This book is based on actual experiences during month-long vacations at a villa rental in the South of France.   Only the identities of the characters have been changed to protect them from the French taxing authorities.

~Ira & Barbara Spector

Foreword

NOWHERE ARE THE DIFFERENCES between French and American cultures more apparent than in the matter of vacations. Americans seek to experience as *much* as possible in the *shortest* amount of time. The French seek to experience as *little* as possible in the *longest* amount of time. Americans do not consider their vacations successful unless they have spent countless hours visiting every museum and learning the history and architecture of every cathedral. The French do not consider their vacations successful unless they have spent countless hours studying the backs of their eyelids.

This description of the French vacation might shock Americans who pass through France on their whirlwind tours of Europe. They see the French, much as themselves, impatient to get things done; they see people who are fueled by cigarettes, coffee and wine; people who are moving, talking and driving as though perpetually late for a very important date.

But visitors who spend more time in France understand what the French are *really* doing. Behind this freneticism is the goal of completing work as efficiently as possible to allow time for a leisurely lunch with wine, aperitifs with friends after work, followed by an unhurried family dinner.

This daily ritual is a mere shadow of the end game, a dress rehearsal for *les grands départs,* a four-to-six-week period when the French, en masse, descend upon resorts and beaches, becoming frozen in time as they pursue *farniente*, which literally translates to "doing nothing," but when achieved equates to peace, tranquility and bliss.

It is telling that Americans have no similar expression. Even more telling is that the closest English synonyms include laziness, loafing and loitering.

This difference in cultural perception explains why French resorts catering to Americans emphasize golf, tennis, sightseeing and every water sport under the sun. By contrast, French resorts catering to their own countrymen promise *farniente*, and focus on lounging on the beach or by the pool. No one is reading or talking. No one is playing volleyball.

Several years ago, my wife and I began spending the entire month of June in the South of France. It all started when Barbara, a lawyer, needed a long break after a particularly acrimonious trial. I enthusiastically supported this notion when she came home one day and threatened to smash her computer into a thousand byte-sized pieces because the hourglass had remained on the screen too long.

In our search for the perfect place to renew my wife, we discovered, purely by accident, that there are numerous affordable villas for rent in the hills along the Mediterranean coast; places where the most important decision we faced was whether to spend the day at the pool and take dinner on the patio, or go to the beach and dine at a seaside restaurant.

But questions arose: Could we as Americans, conditioned by a strict work ethic, actually spend an entire vacation doing nothing? If we did, would we change? Could we actually find peace when we knew little of the language and even less of the culture? And finally, how much would it cost to do nothing?

This is the story of our discovery. This is the story of *farniente*.

~Ira Spector

In Search of "Enchanted April"

WHILE LOOKING FOR a vacation rental in France, my wife and I uncovered the world's greatest travel scam. By telling landlords we were interested in renting their properties for an entire month, Barbara and I were treated royally. Wine flowed, food was served, laughter filled the air. In the ten days we had been in the country, we never had to spring for a major meal.

There were, however, a couple of complications.

The steady diet of rich French food was wreaking havoc with my wife's stomach, and her face had taken on the pallor of yesterday's crème brulée.

The other problem was that every rental we inspected had major shortcomings. Admittedly, we had set the bar quite high, with images of the grand villa we had seen in the movie, "Enchanted April" . . . but on a budget more suitable for a bungalow.

By way of example, the so-called "lovely" and "charming" Parisian apartments that had been carefully culled from catalogs were, in actuality, dingy flats with creaky floors, bare light bulbs dangling from the ceiling, and shelves crammed with kitschy curios.

The "quaint" and "affordable" country homes in the Languedoc region had tiny bedrooms that felt more like jail cells, and ancient kitchens that were perfect for boiling gruel. The only rental with potential was high on a hillside. Although it had a view of the Pyrenees, it was also the location of a large loudspeaker used to broadcast booming news flashes to the villagers below.

The "modern and quiet" dwellings in Provence were in the middle of a large development of cookie cutter homes. Yes, there were views of rolling lavender fields, but one would have to peer through the neighbor's bedroom to see them.

When we reached the point where only three days remained in our vacation, it had become abundantly clear that after thousands of miles traveled and thousands of dollars expended, our dream to find a perfect vacation spot had turned into the perfect nightmare.

Having exhausted ourselves, as well as our list of vacation rentals, we checked into a small hotel south of Aix-en-Provence to recharge before being crushed into coach class for the long flight home. After unpacking, we left our room to explore the grounds when Barbara suddenly collapsed on a bench in front of the hotel's entrance, dropping her forehead into one hand and holding her stomach with the other. "A-r-r-r-g-h," she groaned.

As is customary in our relationship when things aren't going well, it's my wife's job to get as depressed as humanly possible, and it falls upon me to pull her out of it. I usually begin the process by engaging her in pointless conversation.

"Can you believe the autumn light?" I said, joining her on the bench. "It makes the hotel sparkle."

Barbara stared at the ground.

"It was precisely this kind of light that inspired Matisse and Cézanne to turn an ordinary Provençal scene into a richly-drawn tour de force."

Barbara continued to stare at the ground.

"What do you think of this part of the country?"

Silence.

"Maybe we can find something to rent around here."

Silence.

"Something with a mountain view," I said, gesturing to nobody in particular at the rocky cliffs of the Massif de la Ste-Baume in the distance.

Silence.

Obviously, my tact wasn't working this time. I saw one last chance to salvage the situation when the hotel's proprietor emerged from the building and headed toward us. Monsieur Martignon was a handsome, silver-haired gentleman with a perpetual twinkle in his eye and an uncanny resemblance to Maurice Chevalier. I could almost hear him singing, "Thank hea-vun for lee-til girls."

I leaned toward Barbara's ear. "The hotel's proprietor is coming. Perhaps he knows of a home we could rent."

"Forget it," she said, slowly lifting her head. "I'm sick. I'm tired. I'm depressed. I'm finished looking at crummy rentals."

"Bonjour," the proprietor said as he walked by our bench. He glanced at Barbara without reacting to the pale, grim look on her face. He probably thought she was one of his British guests.

I quickly stood. *"Ah, pardonnez-moi, Monsieur."*

The proprietor stopped. "Yes?"

"My wife and I are looking for a home to rent for the month of June. Do you know of anything in this area?"

"Je suis désolé," he replied, shaking his head. "There is nothing around here. But my family owns a vacation villa in the hills above Ste-Maxime, on the Mediterranean coast. The house is *très tranquil.* There

is a view of *la mer* and a private swimming pool. One can walk to the beach just down the hill. Yes, I could rent it to you."

Barbara jerked erect as if jolted by electricity.

"I have pictures of Villa La Chandelle. Would you care to have a look?" he asked.

"Sure," I replied, trying not to get too excited. I figured there would be no way we could afford his family's Mediterranean villa.

We followed Monsieur Martignon into the lobby. He reached behind the reception desk and handed me a packet of photos. Barbara peered over my shoulder as I examined each one. There were three bedrooms and three baths, a dining room, a fireplace, a modern kitchen, a satellite TV room, an infinity swimming pool, and a view of the sea.

"The appliances are new since last year," the hotelier added.

"May I inquire about the rate?" I said, cringing.

"For June I must ask 1000 euros per week. I think this is a good price."

Even in languid Languedoc, it was virtually impossible to find rental properties in that price range. When I was able to get my mouth to work again I managed to say, "Ah . . . is it possible to stay at your villa before we return home? We have three more days."

Monsieur reached in a drawer. "Of course," he said, casually handing me the keys. "It is just two hours from here." He took out a road map and began marking it while Barbara and I glanced at each other, silently communicating our excitement.

We thanked Monsieur Martignon and hurried back to our room. "I'll pack while you find some

Alka-Seltzer for me," Barbara said, suddenly energized. "I have a good feeling about this, and I don't want to be sick any longer than necessary. And buy a few groceries for the villa while you're at it."

I glanced at my watch: it was just after one in the afternoon. "My God, Barbara, it's prime nap time around here. *Nothing's* going to be open."

Barbara picked up a small white bottle. "One more thing: I'll need some eye cream, too—this jar is empty."

"What! Eye cream? You've got to be kidding."

"Keep in mind the label will be in French," she said calmly. "Look for the words *yeux* and *contour de l'oeil.*"

"Gimme the jar!" I said, taking it and storming out.

I had no idea where I was going to find Alka-Seltzer and groceries—much less eye cream. On prior trips to France, not once did I enter a grocery store—plenty of museums, churches and restaurants, yes; grocery stores, no. I wasn't sure if I would recognize a French grocery store if I accidentally tripped and fell into one.

As I drove away, I didn't attempt to look for anything open in the tiny village adjacent to the hotel. Instead, I came to a *rond-point,* a traffic circle, and exited in the direction of Aix-en-Provence, taking a two-lane highway that ran through acres and acres of beautiful Provençal farmland. For ten minutes I was alone on the road. Then suddenly, up ahead, I spotted traffic—lots of it. Cars and light trucks were turning into a giant parking lot with a sprawling building in the center of it. But with the city of Aix still tens

11

of kilometers away, my initial reaction was that the locals must be buying farm equipment here.

I maneuvered into a line of vehicles snaking into the parking lot. If nothing else, it would be a good place to turn around, return to the hotel, and admit defeat. As I approached the massive building, I noticed a large sign with a red and green bird over the word "Auchan." That told me nothing. I parked and watched customers get out of their vehicles and push oversized shopping carts into the main entrance.

What the hell, I thought. I went over to a long row of carts and tugged at one. But it wouldn't budge. On closer inspection I noticed that each cart was chained to the one in front of it through a small rectangular box with a slot for a one-euro coin. I reached into my pocket and slipped the coin into the slot. *Voila!* The chain dropped off, and my giant shopping cart and I were on our way. That was the first time it registered that in spite of all my prior trips to France, I knew next to nothing about the country's infrastructure.

As I entered the main entrance, I still had no clue as to what to expect. But things were looking up when I found myself in a long corridor of clothing boutiques and cafés. I was thinking about getting a cup of coffee when the corridor suddenly opened into the biggest department store I had ever seen. The aisles were so long that they narrowed down to points. Major appliances were on my left, dry goods in front of me, and fresh foods to my right. The superstores now common in the United States came to mind, but they paled in comparison to Auchan.

Stunned, I walked straight ahead. As fate would have it, I found myself in the cosmetic aisle. There was eye cream everywhere. It took a while, but I found the exact formulation Barbara wanted, and I placed the tiny white jar in the center of my enormous shopping cart.

Then I checked my watch. At the rate I had been slogging along, it would take at least three days to get to the good stuff—the wine and the cheese

Twenty minutes later, I pushed my cart toward the checkout lines. There were fifty rows of seated clerks lined up to take money. In fact, that was all they did. Watching for a moment, I learned it was up to the customer to remove the goods from the cart, lay each item on the conveyor belt, and bag it after it was scanned. I joined a line with only a handful of people in front of me, and by the time it was my turn I had the procedure down pat. I confidently placed my purchases on the conveyor and got my credit card ready. The eye cream, wine, bread, cheese, pasta and sauce were scanned without a hitch. But all hell broke loose when it came to the fruit. The clerk, a stern elderly woman with a ruddy complexion and a wart on her cheek, held up my bag of peaches and gestured first at the bag and then at me. The wart bobbled as she said something in rapid-fire French.

I shrugged and blurted, *"Je ne comprends pas."*

The clerk repeated whatever she had said.

Not knowing what else to do, I tried to give her my credit card. She pushed my hand away with her elbow, picked up my bag of plums and said something else, this time a little slower, carefully mouthing her words as if she were talking to a child.

I was clueless.

Then she picked up my pears, dangled them in front of my face and began yelling, her mouth contorted, her eyes wide, the purple veins of her temples bulging. The line behind me was growing longer by the second.

Still holding my credit card, I raised my palms toward the ceiling in placation.

Finally the woman dropped my fruit, looked away in disgust, picked up a microphone, and made an announcement over the loudspeaker. I figured she was telling the entire store what an imbecile I was. Or maybe she was calling security and I would soon be bodily ejected. Or perhaps they would arrest me for touching the fruit—I recalled reading something about a French custom where you pointed to the fruit you wanted, and then someone wearing white gloves would bag it for you. I wondered if I would get one phone call at the *gendarmerie*. I began to sweat as I pictured Barbara basking in the sun by Monsieur Martignon's pool while I sat on a cot in a dark cell deep in the *Bastille*. Perhaps if I threw myself at the mercy of the court I would only be sentenced to a month in Languedoc, in that rental with the booming loudspeaker.

In less than a minute, a young man arrived on rollerblades. He took my fruit and skated away. The old woman held up her hand, signaling for me to wait, probably sensing I was about to make a run for it.

She was right.

But I stood my ground, watching the young man became smaller and smaller as he rollerbladed to a point. Eventually he returned with barcode labels on the bags, and I now understood I was supposed to weigh the fruit and place these labels on the bags before checking out. The clerk scanned the fruits, took my credit card and, in short order, I aimed my cart toward the parking lot and I was on my way.

⟶

"You won't believe what just happened," I told Barbara back in our hotel room. I took the eye cream out of the grocery bag and held it up like a trophy.

"Why were you gone so long?" she asked, ignoring the eye cream and making no effort to hide the irritation in her voice. "I'm anxious to get to the villa while it's still daylight."

"I stumbled upon the French horn of plenty."

"What *are* you talking about?"

"There was this HUGE building in the middle of farmland, and it had a red and green bird logo so I had no—"

"—never mind, tell me on the way."

The Pig Farm

THE MOOD IN THE CAR was gloomy. In my excitement over discovering Auchan, a store with a boundless selection of eye cream and just about everything else, I had forgotten about Barbara's Alka-Seltzer. To make matters worse, as we pressed eastward toward Ste-Maxime and Monsieur Martignon's villa, I had become caught up in the telling of my story and the subtleties of buying French fruit. Consequently, I took a curve too fast and had to hit the brakes, throwing Barbara first sideways and then pitching her forward.

A glance at my wife told me that storytelling time was over.

There is nothing like an angry and sick spouse to cast a pall over the traveling experience. Only a short time ago I was convinced that I had miraculously salvaged our vacation by finding an "Enchanted April" rental, but now I wasn't so sure. What if we had given up a comfortable hotel room for unacceptable accommodations in an unacceptable location? Perhaps Monsieur Martignon had omitted a few details when he described his villa in glowing terms. What if the glow was due to a humming, high-power transmission tower looming over the house?

I had good reason to worry. A year earlier, a similar combination of superlatives and low rent seduced us into taking a "charming stone cottage amidst an olive grove on a farm in Tuscany." Like many before us, we were enthralled by the idea of vacationing in rural Tuscany and making luscious meals out of local ingredients. But the reality was another story. After

17

our flight landed in Pisa and we picked up our rental car, a pintsized Fiat, I promptly became lost. The problem was that in rural Tuscany, by design or laxity, signs are eschewed, making it difficult if not impossible to locate one particular stone cottage in a land where stone cottages dot the hillsides all the way to the horizon.

As the sun began to set, we found ourselves in a tiny village that appeared deserted except for a middle-aged man who was leaning against a pole, puffing on a cigarette. His white polyester shirt was partially unbuttoned, revealing a gold chain. I decided to compromise my manhood and ask him for help.

"Scusi," I said.

The man approached the Fiat. *"Signore?"*

"Parla inglese?" I asked.

"No, Signore," he said shrugging, giving me an apologetic, nicotine-stained smile.

I showed him our booking confirmation with the name of the farm. Recognition filled his eyes and he began pointing and rattling off directions.

I held my hand up. *"Un momento,"* I said, signaling Barbara to climb into the tiny backseat. Then I said, *"Prego,"* and motioned for the man to sit beside me.

Although it didn't seem unusual at the time, the smoking man—without a moment's hesitation—climbed in and we drove off. Then, following his hand signals, I turned onto a narrow rutted trail that took us into heavily canopied woodlands. The sun now touched the horizon, and only a few rays of light filtered through the trees.

Our Samaritan, his cigarette dangling from his mouth, squinted through the smoke and spoke nonstop while continuing to point this way and that. The going was rough, but we made steady progress until we encountered a dense swarm of black flies blocking the road. I braked, the flies engulfed us, and the world went dark. The man cursed, and then pushed on my right leg to gun the engine, parting the insect cloud and allowing us to see again.

"Ecco il podere," the man said pointing. He was referring to a compound of stone houses that slowly appeared in front of us like Brigadoon arising out of a black mist.

I pulled into the driveway and we all piled out of the Fiat. I thanked our guide profusely, but he waved me off when I offered to drive him back to the village. *"Cammino,"* he said. It was dusk, and I assumed he was thinking I would never find the farm again on my own in the dark.

He was right.

As we watched the smoking Samaritan disappear into the black cloud, a British voice behind us said, "You must be the Spectors."

I turned to face a young man of college age. "Yes."

"Did you have much trouble finding us?" he asked. His manner was that of someone who already knew the answer.

"Ah . . . we had a little help," I replied.

"Good move," he said, nodding. "My name is Noland. Please follow me and I'll show you to your cottage." As the young man led us through the compound, we received a history of the property. Noland explained that before his parents bought this farm, it had livestock and olive trees in accordance with the Italian tradition of *coltura promiscua*—promiscuous cultivation. But now only the trees remained.

19

"Where are your parents?" I inquired.

"On holiday in India. Actually, they're away quite a bit."

That should have set off all kinds of bells and whistles, but I was too tired to think it through.

"What kind of livestock?" Barbara asked.

"Pigs," Noland answered casually as he opened the door to our cottage.

That should have set off more bells and whistles. But like most transatlantic travelers who have first been traumatized and paralyzed in coach class, then tenderized by an endless ride in a tiny Fiat with no discernible shock absorbers, we were initially in denial when we found ourselves inhabiting completely unacceptable accommodations.

"Cheers," the young man said as he closed the door.

The first thing we noticed was a methane-like odor pervading the cottage, and my immediate thought was that centuries of continuous pig farming couldn't be erased overnight. And although it was prime feeding time for the mosquitoes and black flies outside, the fumes forced us to open all the windows and invite them in for dinner.

The next thing I noticed were strong hints that we were not the only guests who had been faced with the Hobson's choice of fumes or flies: The white-washed stone walls were adorned with black dots, which, upon closer inspection, weren't a quirk of local interior design, but the remnants of squashed insect bodies.

I dragged our luggage into the small bedroom and turned on the single lamp, its tiny bulb casting a pathetic yellow glow on two single mattresses lying on low wooden platforms. As Barbara went to investigate the source of the odor, I stared at the bag containing the novels we had brought, and wondered how we were going to read them in the dim glow of a nightlight.

"The gas is coming from beneath the floor of the bathroom," Barbara said, "so don't plan on lingering in there. And there's no toilet paper, either. Would you please go out and ask that young man to give us some?"

"Sure," I replied, swatting at a couple of mosquitoes that had been sucking furiously on my neck. "There are probably fewer insects outside."

At the main house, I peered through the screen door and saw Noland sitting in a comfortable chair under a bright reading light. "Excuse me," I said. "We don't have any toilet paper."

The young man looked up but remained seated, showing no interest in inviting me and my mosquitoes inside. "The *podere's* antiquated sewer system can't handle toilet paper," he said casually. "But if you must use any, you'll have to dispose of it in our compost heap." He started to explain how to find it, but I remembered the black flies and told him it wasn't necessary. As I turned to leave, he added, "Think of it as experiencing life in fourteenth-century Tuscany." His tone said I should be grateful for not having to pay extra for the privilege.

Exhausted, we went to bed without dinner, without reading, without unpacking, and without toilet paper. Only the mosquitoes ate that evening.

After a fitful night, we awoke midmorning, and I couldn't tell which was worst: the insect bites; the headache from the gas; or the gnawing in the pit of

my stomach. Our last meal had been a meager breakfast on the flight to Pisa—a year ago it seemed—and
I knew we had better eat soon if we were going to
cope with this disastrous situation.

We quickly dressed and climbed into the Fiat. It
was almost noon by the time we found a parking spot
just outside the wall of a fourteenth-century hilltop
town. Thoughts of a quaint café with outdoor seating, warm pastries, and strong coffee, danced in my
head. Then we would find a grocery store with farm
fresh produce, prime meats, Chianti wines, candles,
and plenty of toilet paper.

But that was not to be.

We quickly learned that the hilltop Tuscans, like
their farming brethren, also eschewed signs. Even
worse, they tucked their commercial establishments
into the most unlikely nooks and crannies of their
walled cities.

Ask a local, "*Dov'è il ristorante?*" and arms and
hands begin to fly. The left arm held up and curved,
and the right hand poking through it, means go under
the arch. The right hand jerking repeatedly toward
the ground means descend the stone staircase. The
left hand slowly moving up and then rapidly curving
down means climb the rampart and leap off the tur-
ret.

We had no choice but to enter the town's Etruscan maze. After a series of twists and turns, we
climbed out of a dark catacomb and actually stumbled
upon a *Trattoria*. But it was closed for lunch.

Their lunch, not *ours*.

I looked around and spotted a middle-aged man
who was leaning out of a second story window,
smoking a cigarette. A gold chain dangled from his

open shirt. He looked like our smoking Samaritan's twin brother. He probably was.

We stepped closer to the window. *"Scusi, Signore, quando è il ristorante aperto?"* I inquired, looking up.

The man grinned. *"Ogni morte di papa."*

"What did he say?" Barbara asked.

"'Every death of a pope.'"

"What?"

"I think he's telling us that the restaurant's hours are set more according to whim than reason."

We were about to resign ourselves to a second foodless day when we got a big break. There was music coming through an archway. We followed the sounds into a plaza where men in matching shorts and suspenders, marching up and down, were blowing trumpets and banging drums.

OOM-PAH-PAH! OOM-PAH-PAH!

Some sort of festival was in progress, but the only food service was from a lonely pizza cart. A grizzled old man sat in the shade of an umbrella, dozing through the din. We woke him and ordered one large pizza each, and when he turned to make our pies, I snatched a bunch of his napkins for use back at the pig farm.

The next day, we searched for food in other hilltop towns, but our timing was off and we were never in the vicinity of a grocery store or a restaurant when a pope had actually died. At one point we did find a grocery, but its iron gate came down with a loud clang just as we arrived. From the back of the store came the clatter of dishes, the clinking of glasses, and the sounds of laughter.

"Look at it this way," I said as we glanced long-ingly through the gate at all the food on the shelves, "if we don't eat, we won't need toilet paper."

"Ha!" Barbara said.

Our hunt for food took us in an ever-widening radius, and by the third day we would have killed for a cheeseburger and French fries. About an hour out from the pig farm, we happened upon a town called Radda in Chianti. But at the top of the hill, instead of a walled Etruscan village, Radda had a modern thor-oughfare lined with shops and restaurants—all of them open. "We died and went to heaven," I whis-tled.

We parked in front of a restaurant, grabbed an outdoor table, and ordered one of everything on the menu. Afterwards, strolling behind bloated stomachs, we came across a four-star hotel. We walked through its elegant lobby and then outside to a swimming pool surrounded by vineyards and rolling hills. "Are you thinking what I'm thinking?" I said to Barbara.

"Yes, let's see if they have a room."

We were in luck. They had one left: a magnificent corner suite with a panoramic view of the vineyards. The catch was they would only hold it until 6:00 p.m., and it was now four in the afternoon. We dashed back to the Fiat and raced to the pig farm. We threw our belongings into our luggage, sat on top of our bags to close them, and jumped into the car.

I paused at the compost heap only long enough to gun the engine and part the cloud of black flies one last time.

A strange gulping sound pulled me back to France and our present journey along the Mediterranean coast. I glanced over at Barbara, whose face had gone from ashen to green. "You'd better stop the car," she warned, rolling down her window.

I pulled over. While my wife collected herself, I checked the map. The nearest town was St-Tropez, which was noteworthy at the time only because it looked large enough to have a pharmacy. We had never been in this part of France, and the name "St-Tropez" had no more significance than "Ste-Maxime" or "St-Raphael" or any other of the hyphenised, beatifically-christened towns that dot the Mediterranean coast.

When Barbara indicated she was able to continue, I followed the road into St-Tropez and parked on a side street. Not surprisingly, like most towns in Provence in the early evening, the streets were empty and the shops closed and shuttered. Only a small sidewalk café was open. "Perhaps a Ginger Ale will help," I suggested.

We took a table outside and ordered. Then in my best French, which sounds like Inspector Clouseau in the "Pink Panther," I asked the waiter, *"Monsieur, où est la pharmacie?"*

The man pointed to the rear entrance of the café and gestured to the left. *"À gauche, Monsieur."*

I turned to Barbara. "I'll be right back." I stood and exited the café, and turned onto a narrow cobblestone street with sidewalks as wide as my shoulders. The sun was low in the sky and the closeness of the buildings cast deep shadows around me. A motor scooter whizzed by and I pressed myself against the wall.

Suddenly the narrow street opened into a vast and brightly-lit movie set. At least that was my first impression. To my left was a harbor filled with multi-million-dollar yachts; to my right were pastel-colored buildings, awash in sunlight and standing in bold relief against an impossibly blue sky. The waterfront scene reminded me of Portofino in Italy, but much more expansive.

Between the harbor and the pastel buildings was a broad esplanade with hundreds of people promenading in front of luxurious yachts or sitting at sidewalk cafés, drinking aperitifs. Clearly, while most of Provence was winding down for the evening, St-Tropez was gearing up.

For a while, I walked along a row of street artists at the harbor's edge, admiring their oils and watercolors. The hum of activity on a nearby yacht grabbed my attention, and I watched crewmembers in dress whites set up an elaborate dinner on a mahogany afterdeck.

Then I remembered Barbara.

I quickly scanned the shopping arcade behind the sidewalk cafés and spotted the pharmacy. I made the purchase and hurried back to my wife. She was holding her head in her hands.

"I have your Alka-Seltzer," I said excitedly.

Barbara lifted her head. "You were gone a long time," she snapped. "Again!"

"You'll never guess what happened."

"This is getting to be a habit with you—don't tell me; you found the biggest pharmacy in the entire world. Then you accidentally stumbled into the aisle with ten thousand flavors of Alka-Seltzer. Let's have it."

"Actually, it's much better than that," I said, handing her the package. "I can't wait to show you."

Barbara downed the medicine while I paid the bill. It took some effort, but I persuaded her to follow me into the dark and narrow street. "Now close your eyes. Trust me."

"This had better be good."

"Trust me."

Barbara closed her eyes. I took her hand and guided her along the narrow sidewalk and into the esplanade. "Okay, you can look now," I said, turning to watch her face as she blinked in the bright sunshine.

"Wow," she exhaled. "You've got to be kidding."

"Can you believe this?" I said.

"You've got to be kidding."

I showed Barbara the cafés, the portside artists, and the luxury yachts. We were both mesmerized by the scene and wanted to remain, but we reluctantly pulled ourselves away from St-Tropez so we could locate the villa before nightfall.

On the drive to Ste-Maxime I said, "You have to admit that things are looking up." My earlier optimism had returned, and I was now grinning like the Cheshire cat.

"We haven't seen the villa yet," Barbara replied, not one to indulge in premature back patting.

"Well, if the place is even *half* as great as it sounds, we're set. We can spend most of our time in St-Tropez."

Monsieur Martignon's directions were good, and twenty minutes later we turned off the coast road and into a neighborhood of attractive hillside homes. The sign on a high wrought iron gate said "Villa La Chandelle." I unlocked the gate and swung it open.

On a plateau rising gently above us, amid a grove of massive *parasol pines*, was a house constructed of beige stucco. It had a red-tile roof in the classic Provençal style and faced the Mediterranean. There was a bedroom at the end of each private wing with French doors that opened to a lawn sloping down to the infinity pool. Flowers were everywhere. We stood on the patio and watched sailboats with colorful spinnakers returning to St-Tropez for the evening.

Villa La Chandelle was simply but tastefully decorated. The walls were white and the floors were tiled with terracotta pavers. The master bedroom had a king-sized, four-poster bed. The kitchen was fully equipped with new appliances, as Monsieur Martignon had represented. There was a large American refrigerator, a radar range and convection oven, a microwave, and a dishwasher and clothes washer. There were abundant cooking utensils and Limoges china.

From the groceries I had purchased at Auchan, I prepared a simple spaghetti dinner while Barbara unpacked, and we dined on the patio, watching the orange glow of sunset deepen into red. A candle flickered on the table and jazz from Riviera Radio floated out of the satellite TV room.

With our senses heightened, my simple meal seemed exquisite. Although only eight hours had passed since I had casually queried Monsieur Martignon about a vacation rental, it felt like a lifetime.

"I can't believe we actually did it," I said, breaking the silence. "And there's plenty of toilet paper."

Barbara sniffed the air. "And no methane gas."

"And not a black fly in sight."

"To *our* 'Enchanted April,'" Barbara toasted, raising her wineglass to mine.

The French Connection

AFTER RETURNING TO CALIFORNIA, the question of how much to take for our month in the South of France was a source of much debate. Barbara's notion of packing was one bikini and a toothbrush. My idea was to take the entire inventory of Circuit City.

"Don't you want to listen to the music of your choice?" I asked early in our deliberations.

"No."

"A subwoofer will give us the full range of bass from our CDs."

"I don't care."

"And wouldn't you like to watch first-run movies on DVDs after dinner?"

"Read my lips . . . N-O."

"Look, e-mail is essential; we can stay in contact and it'll save us a *ton* in long distance telephone charges."

"NO!"

This was pretty much the way it went until a few weeks before our departure date. Barbara finally relented, knowing that it was impossible to reason with a gadget lunatic beset by a deeply-rooted fear of becoming bored. So the deal we hammered out was this: We would take no more than two carryons and five suitcases. If I could cram a laptop computer, a heavy voltage transformer, a subwoofer with satellite speakers, and an inflatable kayak into our luggage, fine. But *I* had to pack and carry *all* of it.

As a trial run, I arranged the seven empty bags on the floor of our bedroom and proceeded to stack all of my absolutely essential items neatly atop the bed. But before long, the pile neared ceiling height, and was listing dangerously. It was clear that no matter how many pairs of socks I crammed into my shoes, all of this junk was not going to fit.

Something would have to go.

I promptly discarded Barbara's bikini and her toothbrush. My rationale was that these things could be purchased in St-Tropez, but I was less certain about the subwoofer.

My goal was to import enough technology to transform the villa's TV room into a small home theater with surround sound. To do this, I would have to play DVD movies through our laptop and feed them into the villa's 35-inch television. This wouldn't be easy since our computer's video signal was incompatible with the French television system.

French television is just one example of why U.S. tourists must bring a suitcase full of special converters if they want to plug anything American into anything French. In the case of television broadcasts, the government of the Republic believes that its citizens deserve nothing less than the best TV picture possible. They consider NTSC, America's fifty-year-old broadcast standard, to be obsolete and scurrilously refer to it as "Never Twice the Same Color." Instead, they created a new broadcast standard from scratch called SECAM. In reality, SECAM is only a standard in France—as well as Iraq, Iran and a few other third-world countries—which adopted it for the sole purpose of preventing their citizens from being corrupted by "I Love Lucy" reruns. For this reason, our own government facetiously characterizes SECAM as a "System Essentially Contrary to the American Method."

After I had located an NTSC-to-SECAM converter and collected everything else I needed for the home theater project, it was time for Phase II—transforming the villa into a high-tech communications center. But before I went too far, I thought it prudent to share my plans with Barbara.

I found my wife in the bedroom, resting after a hard day at work. Her eyes were closed so I wasn't certain if she were actually listening to me, which isn't uncommon whenever I'm chatting about computers and technology.

". . . so, when we're not using the laptop for the home theater," I was saying, "I'll connect it to the villa's phone line so we can send and receive faxes. We can even have voicemail. Just think, when someone calls they'll hear, '*Bonjour,* you have reached the Spectors at Villa La Chandelle. If you know your party's extension, dial it now. For *la piscine*, press 1. For *la cuisine,* press 2. For *la salle de bains* press 3. For other options, press 0.'"

There was no immediate reaction from my wife. Perhaps she was asleep.

". . . and we can sign up with a local Internet Service Provider and surf the Web, trade stocks, and pay bills. I can also establish a virtual private network, so you can connect directly to your law firm's intranet."

Barbara sprang up as if I had thrown cold water in her face. She was staring wide-eyed at me. "Ira, we need to talk." She patted the bed next to her and said, "Sit."

I sat.

"Let me ask you a question. Do you want to do these things simply because you can, or are you afraid of becoming disconnected from the technology that gives you your identity?"

I thought for a second. "U-m-m."

"Aren't we taking a month off from the complexities of life here to give ourselves an opportunity to relax and develop a fresh perspective?" Her tone was soft and even, as if talking to a mental patient.

"Yes."

"Then why do you want to import this life into that one?"

"I guess I got a little carried away."

"Well, if you don't want to see *me* carried away, then we need to put a stop to all of this"—her voice was rising. "I will not travel thousands of miles just so I could telecommute and pretend I had never left my office!" She was shouting now.

"Okay, okay, forget about the virtual private network."

My wife narrowed her eyes into slits.

"Okay, no voicemail, either."

"You still don't get it, do you?"

"Actually, I do get it. I really do. I'll leave the laptop at home. And no CDs, or DVDs either; it'll just be *toi et moi*."

Barbara turned and stared at the wall. I figured she was trying to picture villa life with just *moi*, and no music and movies.

She finished ruminating and returned to me. "The problem with the damn laptop is that it can do too much. If we bring it—and I mean *if*—we'll need to establish some strict rules."

"Okay," I said.

We started our negotiations simply, with music as the first agenda item. Barbara admitted that songs floating out of the villa would add to our enjoyment. We could have Pavarotti join us for breakfast at the pool; jazz fill idyllic afternoons; and depending on the evening's menu and mood, the sweetness of Billie Holiday or the salsa of Ricky Martin.

The alternative was the local radio programming we had listened to last September. The station out of St-Tropez transmitted a loud and thumping disco beat, interspersed with a shrieking announcer. Other stations used a talk show format with callers debating the merits of wild herb body exfoliation, or some other esoteric *sujet du jour.*

Only Riviera Radio, an English-language station out of Monaco, offered hope. By evening, the broadcast switched from British expatriates and yachtsmen chatting about the stock market, to jazz and big band sounds. Programs were occasionally interrupted by special announcements informing listeners that they were about to be stranded again by a French railroad or airline strike. But the station's distant location made its reception unreliable.

Score one for the laptop, which could play hours of our favorite MP3 music and CDs.

The next item on the agenda was movies.

The alternative to viewing our own chosen films was French television. Nightly programming included dubbed reruns of "Cheers," with Cliff and the other barflies chiming *"Bonsoir, Norm!"* in unison. Other choices included game shows where contestants in clown costumes threw food at each other as the audience laughed hysterically. Thanks to SECAM, we could watch these broadcasts in the clearest picture possible.

For serious viewing we had the choice of the nightly news, where irate commentators tore mercilessly into government officials, or soccer matches, where irate fans tore mercilessly into each other.

Score another one for the laptop.

Then things got a bit trickier. "I'm throwing faxes on the table," I said.

"Ha! Over my dead and lifeless body."

"Hold on—I'm not talking about faxes for work; I'm talking about communicating with Monsieur Martignon. A fax from the villa will give me the opportunity to frame my question carefully, and I can even use the laptop to translate the text into French."

"Ha! The last time you tried that he told you the computer spoke French like a sick cow."

This went on for a while, but we got through it when my attorney-wife had me sign an agreement specifying that I would "engage in the activity of faxing only for the express limited purpose of communicating with the landlord."

Now we were down to our last and most difficult agenda item: the Internet. This was a subject of extreme delicacy since I didn't want to reveal that my body had been invaded by an alien life form known as the "Creeping Feature Creature," which mainly seeks out techies and manifests its presence by forcing the host to continually add technological complexities to his life.

"Well," I started gently, "as long as the laptop has to be connected to the phone line for faxing, I think we should give Internet access some consideration."

"ANGST!" Barbara shouted.

"Wait . . . we can restrict it to retrieving information relevant to our vacation."

Barbara put her fingers in her ears and squeezed her eyes shut. But she remained silent. I took that as an encouraging sign.

"You can get weather forecasts," I offered, deliberately pushing one of her hot buttons. My wife loved to check the weather over the Net.

Barbara removed her fingers from her ears. "What about e-mail?" she asked, baiting me.

I didn't bite. "Absolutely no e-mail. The Net will just be used to gather information on local events, museum schedules, maps, restaurant ratings— whatever. And I promise not to log on without parental supervision."

Barbara sighed. "All right."

The meeting was concluded and we retired for the evening. As I edged toward sleep, I basked in the knowledge that we had resolved a dicey "men are from Mars and women are from Venus" issue. I had gotten most of what I wanted, and the Creeping Feature Creature was satisfied for the time being.

But deep inside of me an ember of humanity still glowed, and I was troubled about the business we had just concluded. Perhaps Barbara's vision of a pure "Enchanted April" vacation was correct. Perhaps our time in the South of France would be compromised by technology. Perhaps I could muster the courage to bring nothing but a bathing suit and a toothbrush.

The idea was provocative, and I fell asleep warmed by the thought of the beaches I had read about near St-Tropez, where one could even leave the bathing suit at home.

The Lime-Green Peugeot

THE RED-EYE out of New York banked for its final approach into Côte d'Azur airport. It was a glorious June morning, and the beach was dotted with sun worshippers, just as I had remembered.

Nearly twenty-four hours after we departed California, Barbara and I sleepwalked with fellow passengers into Nice's international terminal. A customs official eyed me suspiciously as I pushed a large pile of luggage brimming with electronic gear through the "Nothing to Declare" exit.

The line for rental cars moved with agonizing slowness because there was only one agent behind the counter, and she was going to great lengths to fill out short forms. Barbara sat on the luggage while I waited the better part of an hour for my turn. By then, I lacked the energy to complain when I was handed the keys to a diesel-powered, subcompact, lime-green Peugeot.

When we finally emerged from the terminal, the world outside was far different than the one in which we had landed. The sky, instead of cloudless and brilliant blue, was dark and ominous. A cold wind lashed down from the Esterel Mountains and sent shivers through my body.

The clouds released their payload just as we reached the Peugeot. Swollen raindrops pelted my face and broke into rivulets that ran down my shirt collar. I stuffed what I could of the luggage into the car's miniscule trunk and the rest I piled onto the backseat.

With Barbara the designated navigator, I cranked the engine and it sputtered to life. I wiped my face with my shirtsleeve, grabbed the steering wheel with both hands, and took a deep breath. All I could think about was the nap I would take at the villa, about an hour's drive from the airport. Then I would connect the laptop to the speakers, and fire up the subwoofer.

Life would be good.

Well, not quite.

The Peugeot had fogged up, its defroster pitifully ineffective against the streams of vapor wafting from our luggage and clothing. Seeing no reasonable way to drive under these conditions, I reluctantly left the shelter of the car, and dashed through the monsoon to *la cabine,* the rental car company's kiosk in the parking lot. Behind the counter was an immaculately coifed middle-aged blonde woman who was busy doing nothing. It has been said that when French women reach middle age, a preprogrammed genetic sequence is triggered, and their naturally-straight brown hair turns blonde and permanently styles itself into an elegant, shoulder-length cut. It remains exactly this way for the remainder of their lives.

"Pardonnez-moi," I said, "do you know how long this storm is expected to continue?"

She considered me over her half-glasses. "Perhaps for ten minutes . . . perhaps for an hour . . . perhaps all day. It is difficult to say."

"Can I have another car?" I inquired. "The Peugeot's defroster is weak."

Her eyes narrowed. "There are no more cars."

"I see. Then can you tell me if the weather might be better in Ste-Maxime? My wife and I have had a long flight and we're anxious to get to our villa." I threw in the villa remark in the hope it would have cachet, and she would treat me like the rich and famous people who routinely deplane at Nice.

She didn't buy it. The rich and famous don't drive around in lime-green Peugeots with ineffectual defrosters.

"Perhaps," she said shrugging and returning to doing nothing.

Now I had done it. I had used up my allotment of three stupid tourist questions.

Back at the Peugeot, Barbara had been busy making circles in the fogged up windshield. I climbed in and made a squishing sound as I settled into the driver's seat. I sighed as I watched my wife's portholes fog up again.

"Let's get out of here," I said. "As long as we hug the coastline and follow the signs to Ste-Maxime, we'll make it to the villa okay."

With Barbara rapidly wiping circles on the inside, and the Peugeot's wipers slowly swishing on the outside, we crawled out of the airport. But following the coastline wasn't as simple as I had thought. Somehow I wound up on La Provençale, the high-speed inland toll road. Although billed as the most efficient way to travel between Nice and Aix-en-Provence, the real function of La Provençale is to provide French drivers with a hair-raising, spine-tingling, death-defying, amusement park ride. This is *exactly* the one place you do not want to be when the visibility is measured in inches, the road is flooded, your tires are aquaplaning, and the safest top speed is 18 mph.

Meanwhile, the French were swerving around us at 200 kilometers per hour as they pretended to be competing at Le Mans. In self-defense I hugged the

41

far right shoulder of the highway. Even the road kill floating in the run-off were moving faster than we were.

Although absolutely terrified, there just wasn't any safe place to pull over. And it didn't help matters when we encountered a horrible four-car wreck. The accident had been so bad it was almost impossible to tell where one car ended and the next began. Through Barbara's dim portholes all we could make out was an accordion of mangled, smoking metal. But I was fairly certain the car in front had once been a lime-green Peugeot.

I slogged along in first gear with my teeth clenched, shoulders hunched, waiting for Jean-Paul Andretti in his Citroen, his beret tilted smartly, a Marlboro dangling from his mouth, to plow into us at any second.

Suddenly a toll plaza appeared. I was never so happy to have to pay money in my entire life. It meant the crazy French drivers would have to slow down and probably even stop. As we approached the plaza, I saw a parking area on the far side and breathed a sigh of relief. Barbara saw it too, so conversation wasn't necessary; we both knew we would pay the toll, park, and wait out the storm. If we had to sit in a fogged-up, lime-green Peugeot for three days until the rain stopped, so be it.

There were about a dozen toll booths in front of us. In the downpour I couldn't distinguish among them, so I simply selected one with a green light overhead. But I had chosen badly. By the time I realized the booth was automated and took only coins, another car was inches from our rear bumper and the driver was gunning his engine.

We were trapped.

Although I had traded dollars for euros during our layover in New York, all I had was paper money because foreign exchange people never bother with coins. Not knowing what else to do, I took out a ten-euro note, rolled down the window, and held it out. Why I did this I do not know. Perhaps I was thinking lightening would strike and magically change my note into *pièces de monnaie*. Or perhaps I was just trying to show the drivers lining up behind me that I wasn't a euro-less slacker. Ignorant maybe, but not euro-less.

As I waved the money, I noticed something was different. On the other side of the plaza, the sky was becoming brighter and the rain was tapering off as if the toll station marked the boundary of the storm front. If only we could escape to the other side I was certain we would be greeted by blue sky, chirping birds, and Judy Garland singing "Somewhere Over the Rainbow."

A *gendarme* approached and I rolled down my window as he leaned toward me. The officer must have seen the growing line of cars and came over to investigate. "Americans," I blurted, as if that explained everything.

He nodded, took the note over to a human toll taker, and returned with change. I could have kissed his boots.

The arm lifted and we were off. I eased the Peugeot all the way up to 36 mph, which, for us, was smoking. As the kilometers ticked off and the sky grew brighter, the monsoon, the mangled wreckage, and the trouble at the tollbooth, all faded into distant memories.

After another forty minutes, Barbara and I pulled up to the gates of Villa La Chandelle. By now, the sun was shining brightly and the air was warm. Through the wrought iron gate the aquamarine water of the infinity pool beckoned. The nightmarish drive had sapped my last reserves of energy, and I was now thinking that after my nap I'd take a nice swim before I began unpacking and hooking up the electronics. There was, however, one slight problem: We were locked out.

The key, which was supposed to be hidden under a large rock to the right of the gate, wasn't there. To make matters worse, the surrounding houses were shuttered as tightly as they had been last fall, eliminating the possibility of asking a neighbor to assist us.

I couldn't believe this was happening. Before we left California, Monsieur Martignon had assured me by fax that the key would be under the rock, and the villa would be ready to receive us. In near panic, we scrambled around the gate area, leaving no stones unturned. But all we found were nocturnal insects scurrying from the light.

Our only option was to telephone the landlord. I prayed there had been no mix-up over our arrival date. We stuffed our bodies back into the Peugeot and drove down the hill, turning onto the coastal road.

I found a public telephone booth. But the irony was that although I now had a pocket full of coins from the toll plaza incident, I couldn't find any place to insert them. There was, however, a slot for credit cards. I picked up the receiver, heard a dial tone, and inserted my MasterCard. The telephone beeped loudly and a display said, *"ANOMALIE."* I tried pressing "0" for the operator. Nothing. I wondered how we would ever achieve any sort of peace in this country when we couldn't even manage a simple call from a phone booth.

I spotted a small hotel across the road and we dragged ourselves inside to ask for help. Behind the reception desk was an elderly woman with blonde hair coifed in the official French matron style. But unlike the rental agent, she greeted us with a warm smile.

"Parlez-vous anglais?" I croaked hopefully.

She looked apologetic and shook her head no.

"Pouvez-vous nous aider?" I said, asking for help. Although my mind was on autopilot, I somehow managed to retrieve this sentence from the list of emergency French phrases I had memorized along with other critically-important expressions such as "more wine," "no anchovies," and "where's the toilet?"

The woman said something I didn't catch. Fortunately Barbara still had her wits about her and simply handed our landlord's phone number to the woman.

"Téléphonez, s'il vous plaît?" I asked, taking the cue.

"Oui, Monsieur," she said, picking up the phone and dialing. She handed me the receiver and I found myself talking to Monsieur Martignon's wife. Actually, Madame Martignon was doing all the talking, in rapid-fire French of course. Although her husband had a fair knowledge of English, I quickly discovered that his wife was predisposed to lengthy soliloquies in her native tongue.

"Où est Monsieur Martignon?" I kept asking every time she paused to take a breath. To her credit, she replied in at least seven different ways, and I finally understood that her husband was on his way and we

were to wait for him in front of the villa. At least that's what I hoped she had said.

By the time we arrived back at the gate I had formulated a plan. "I'll climb over first," I told Barbara. "Then I'll help you over and we can crash on the lawn until Monsieur Martignon shows up."

"You mean *if* he shows up."

I scrabbled on top of the Peugeot's roof and gingerly eased one leg over the gate's pointy tops. I had visions of slipping, and then trying to explain my injuries to a local doctor. I made a mental note to add, "I have accidentally changed my sex" to my personal list of emergency French phrases.

But I made it to the other side intact, helped Barbara over, and soon she was asleep on the lawn. I, too, desperately wanted to nap, but I was afraid that when the landlord drove up and didn't see anyone, there was no telling what he might do.

The sun was lowering in the sky when I heard a car pull up. I hurried down the driveway. Through the gate I saw Monsieur Martignon get out of his car and stop to stare at the Peugeot. He turned when he heard me approach. "I see you are already inside," he said.

"Ah . . . we couldn't find the key," I explained. I suddenly worried he might view our climbing over the gate as trespassing. I prayed we hadn't committed a *faux pas* that would cause him to bodily eject us from his property.

Instead the landlord casually unlocked the gate, swung it open, and handed me the key. "And Madame Spector, I trust she is well?"

"Oh yes, she's fine," I said, pointing to her sprawled, lifeless form on the lawn.

Monsieur Martignon turned back to the Peugeot. "I have not seen a color like this before on *une voiture*. She is *très unique*. I think you will have no trouble finding her in the parking lot," he remarked.

"The key wasn't under the rock," I said, not yet ready to let go of the matter.

"Yes, that is because I was bringing it to you. But first it was necessary to stop and buy new light bulbs for the guest bedroom." His facial expression told me the subject was closed.

"Uh-huh," I said, too tired to argue.

"Now I must be on my way. *Bonnes vacances,*" Monsieur Martignon said as he climbed into his car and drove off, leaving me holding the bag of light bulbs.

"The Proper Taste of Spaghetti Water"

THE NEXT DAY, I was just beginning the process of unpacking my electronics gear when Barbara came over. "You should learn the villa's systems before you even *think* about those gadgets of yours," she cautioned. "There are strange controls and switches everywhere, and it could be very costly if we pushed the wrong button and damaged something." She went on to explain that French law operates under a presumption of innocence similar to the United States. "But Americans," she added, "are guilty no matter what."

I had to admit that the amount of technology used to operate the villa was impressive. At the push of a button, a motorized steel shutter sealed off the front entrance, *à la* James Bond. A computerized heating system controlled the temperature of the pipes running under the floor tiles. Another system controlled the sprinkling system zones. A large propane tank fed a complex hot water system for the house and the swimming pool. Proximity detectors turned security lights on and off. I assumed that all of this was necessary because of the large amount of time the villa remained unoccupied.

Clearly, we wouldn't have a peaceful vacation if we worried about innocently pushing the wrong button and accidentally flooding the place, blowing it up, or burning it down.

Armed with my pocket dictionary, I decided to tackle the swimming pool's control room first. I opened a door to a concrete bunker full of switches, valves, dials and digital displays. It reminded me of the bridge of the Starship Enterprise.

On the wall was a large sign labeled:

"RECOMMANDATIONS IMPORTANTES."

It went on to say:

"NETTOYER LE PANIER À FEUILLES DANS LE BAC TAMPON."

According to my dictionary this meant:

"CLEAN THE BASKET HAS LEAVES IN THE VAT BUFFER."

I carefully examined the maze of pipes, valves and filters to see if I could discern anything that resembled a "vat buffer." No luck. I was about to look outside when I noticed one of the displays flashing a warning message:

"MANQUE DE SEL . . . MANQUE DE SEL."

This I understood. The pool wanted salt. Salt? Suddenly it dawned on me that the water purifying system relied on ordinary salt, which explained why the strong chlorine odor of swimming pools in America wasn't apparent here. It was a good thing, too, since we would not have been able to enjoy our poolside breakfast with chlorine fumes wafting around us, and if the doves, squirrels and other creatures who sipped the water were staggering around and falling over dead.

I noticed a large white bag in the corner of the room labeled, *"Sel de la Piscine."* It was full of large pellets the size of campfire marshmallows. A plastic bucket sat next to the bag. But did I throw a handful of pellets into *la piscine*? A bucket full? The entire bag?

Not wanting to risk ruining an expensive filtering system, I went back to the house and called Monsieur Martignon. "The pool is demanding salt," I said, after the usually pleasantries.

He sighed heavily. "*La piscine,* always *manque de sel, manque de sel!* She is like my wife, never satisfied." Monsieur went on to talk about Madame, in his usual language soup of English and French.

Talking to our landlord in person had not been a problem since I understood the gist of the conversation by watching hand gestures and facial expressions. Over the telephone, however, I was only catching part of what he was saying—the part in English.

"But what is the quantity of salt I should give to her . . . I mean . . . *la piscine?"* I asked, attempting to steer the conversation away from Madame Martignon and back to the matter-at-hand.

There was a long pause. I figured Monsieur Martignon was trying to think of a way to instruct me in English. Finally, he said, "Do you know the proper taste of spaghetti water?"

"Y-yes," I replied, beginning to see where this was going. I imagined myself chucking in marshmallow-sized salt pellets, stirring them with an enormous wooden spoon, and sipping the pool water.

"Well, not quite so much."

"Okay," I said, thanking him and hanging up. It suddenly dawned on me that living in a French villa was going to take much more effort than I had envisioned. I now understood the reason Monsieur Martignon's rent was relatively low was that the care and feeding of the pool, and the tending of the flowers, the lawn, and the rest of the villa, would rest squarely on our shoulders. Monsieur Martignon had shrewdly acquired two live-in caretakers who were paying him for the privilege.

But we didn't mind. Over the next couple of days I actually enjoyed puzzling out the villa's systems. I even enjoyed the more mundane tasks of gardening and sweeping the pool. Barbara, too, seemed at peace as she went about her housekeeping chores.

By the third day, a couple of special things occurred. The first was that I no longer thought about what was happening back home. The second was that our garbage toter was badly overflowing. This made me reflect on how much villa life contrasted with staying at a hotel, how hotels go to great lengths to shelter guests from life in the real world, and how one can never truly *experience* life in a foreign country until one knows what to do with the garbage. I wondered if a truck came to our street and hauled it away. The surrounding villas were shuttered, so there was no example to follow, no one to ask. Perhaps we were supposed to take it somewhere. But where? I didn't relish the idea of driving around with several days of trash stuffed into the Peugeot's tiny trunk.

"Do you know what we're supposed to do with *la gar-BAGE?*" I asked Barbara on the off-chance she might have seen a trash truck go by.

"Non, mon cher," she replied, practicing her French. "Why don't you call Monsieur Martignon?"

I glanced at the overflowing toter, trying to think of a way to avoid calling the landlord again. I was reluctant to bother him with such an inane inquiry, figuring there would be many more questions to come, and I didn't want him to think he had rented his high-tech vacation villa to a pair of ingénues. "Monsieur, what shall I do with *la gar-BAGE?*" I imagined myself asking him. After his previous instruction regarding the salt and the pool water, God only knows what he would tell me to do with it.

"What are you waiting for?" Barbara asked. *"Allez-y!"*

I took a deep breath and walked over to the phone. Barbara sat nearby with a dictionary, ready to translate English into French whenever I got in over my head, which would probably be whenever the conversation went beyond *"Bonjour."*

"I have a question about *la gar-BAGE,*" I said when the landlord came to the phone.

"What?" he asked. "I do not understand you."

"Does a truck come for *la gar-BAGE?*"

"What? I do not understand."

I sighed and looked at Barbara.

"Ask him, 'What day?'" she suggested. "Try *'quel jour?'*"

"*La gar-BAGE, Monsieur, quel-jour-pour-le-truc?*" I inquired, carefully enunciating each word.

"I do not understand."

Barbara was trying to get my attention.

"Ah, just a moment," I said, covering the mouthpiece.

"No, no, Ira. *Truc* in French means 'trick.'" She was furiously turning pages. "Use *'le camion.'*"

I went back to Monsieur Martignon. "*Le camion pour la gar-BAGE? Quel jour?*"

"I do not understand."

I dropped my forehead into my hand. I was beginning to think that perhaps the problem was with the word *garbage*. I tried a synonym. "*Re-FUSE, re-FUSE,*" I insisted in Clouseau-talk.

Barbara was turning pages and waving her arms at me. "No, no, *'refuse'* means 'deny' in French. You've just started an argument with him! The correct phrase for 'the garbage' is *'les ordures.'*"

"No, sir, I do not refuse," Monsieur Martignon replied. "I simply do not understand you."

The landlord was getting angry with me. I figured at any moment he would demand satisfaction and challenge me to a duel. I wondered if the Provençaux used swords or pistols at twenty paces.

"I'm very sorry, Monsieur," I said hastily. "*Les ordures? Quel-jour-pour-le-camion?*" I asked hopefully.

"*Tous les jours!*" Monsieur replied.

"Everyday?"

"Of course. Is it not the same in America?"

"No, it's picked up only once a week."

There was silence on the other end. I pictured Monsieur Martignon shaking his head and rolling his eyes. Finally he said, "Does it not stink?"

"I suppose," I said, feeling about one-inch tall.

Later, as I stationed the toter outside the gate, I reflected on the lessons I had learned. First, I was grateful we had rented a villa from an individual who knew some English—I shuddered to think of the trouble we would be in if French was the only way we could communicate with our landlord; and second, I vowed never to substitute English words when attempting to speak French unless I was certain of their meaning.

For example, I will never again ask a waiter for *"Un Coke avec limon."* *Citron* is the correct word for lemon.

Limon means slime.

The Politeness of Patou

THE DAY OFFICIALLY BEGAN when we opened the French doors and stepped outside. There was no need to wear robes. Our only neighbors were the white doves sipping from the pool, the brown squirrels scurrying up the *parasol pine* trees and, on occasion, a family of wild boar that had been busy digging up the lawn. Our sudden appearance would spook the piglets and they would trot off with dad. But mom stood her ground until her family was a safe distance away, holding us hostage with loud grunts, sharp teeth, and her best eat *merde* and die look.

Our morning ritual was to throw on shorts and shirts, and take breakfast by the pool. But first I drove down the hill to pick up *USA Today* and any groceries we needed, while Barbara brewed the coffee, chose the music, and set the table.

My initial stop was Le Petit Casino, a small, well-stocked grocery store on the coast road. The first time I shopped there I was pleasantly surprised by the familiarity of the products. I was pleasantly surprised because I didn't want to stand in an aisle with a pocket dictionary in one hand, a strangely-wrapped package in the other, trying to determine if I were buying *poisson* or *poison*. Instead I zipped right along, filling my cart with Florida orange juice, American cereals, espresso coffee, wine, croissants, fresh fruits, and vegetables.

I was also surprised to see a variety of low-fat and nonfat foods. There was lean hamburger meat, skinless chicken and even reduced-fat cheeses. What happened to the French paradox, I wondered? What happened to the promise of a healthy life as long as fat-laden meals were washed down with copious amounts of red wine? Here was a paradox within a paradox, but I was too busy discovering exquisitely sinful ingredients to worry about it.

Only a few French products were noticeably different: Fresh eggs were brown in color, the yogurt lacked sweeteners, and the milk wasn't refrigerated. This last discovery surprised me until I remembered that Pasteur was a great French scientist who knew what he was doing. In any event, the milk was delicious, even at room temperature, and even in the *écrèmé,* or skim, variety.

On that very first shopping trip, my cart was overflowing with groceries, cleaning materials, and all the other items we needed to set up housekeeping. In order to avoid another fruit *faux pas,* I carefully studied the checkout process. But shopping at Le Petit Casino was simpler than at Auchan: all I had to do was bag the groceries after they were weighed and scanned by the clerk.

Unfortunately, I encountered an unexpected problem. Due to the region's dry climate, there was a great deal of static electricity in the air, and the thin plastic grocery bags that the clerk handed me simply would not open. I tried to separate the edges with my fingernails without success. I wet my fingertips and the bag still refused to open. I vigorously rubbed the two sides together and *le sac* flew up and stuck to my face.

Meanwhile, the pile on the counter grew higher and the line behind me grew longer. To make matters worse, while I seemed to be purchasing supplies for a small army, the other customers were merely buying baguettes.

I had no choice but to continue rubbing like a madman. The clerk, looking amused, began handing me items that no longer fit on the counter. With both arms full and no way to open a plastic bag, I had a sudden flash of Le Petit Casino brilliance: I could simply place the scanned items back into the cart, pay the clerk, grab some plastic bags on the way out, and leisurely pack my purchases in the privacy of the Peugeot.

The next stop was usually Le Tabac, the town's news and smoke shop. However, buying *USA Today* turned into a hit or miss proposition because only one copy was allocated to the store. So I made an arrangement with the shopkeeper to hide the paper under the counter for me. French proprietors have a propensity for remembering and favoring repeat customers, so special arrangements are readily effected. It was gratifying to walk into Le Tabac, be instantly recognized, and have the counter person reach down and hand me the newspaper as I walked up.

But this special treatment came with a price—I was expected to chat. Pleasantries such as *"Bonjour,"* *"Ça va?"* and *"Bonne journée,"* which worked well everywhere else, were not sufficient under the rules of engagement at Le Tabac, rules that required a conversation about the weather, my plans for the day, and a discussion about life in California—all in cheerful and rapid-fire French, and all before my first cup of Barbara's coffee.

I tried to comply and even practiced in front of the mirror. Although my year of college French was helpful, there were times when I was stymied because the Provençaux speak in a drawl, running words together like American Southerners, so that even familiar French expressions were sometimes incomprehensible.

The person with whom I most frequently performed the Tabac ritual was Patou, the twenty-something daughter of the owners. One morning, still half asleep, I trudged over to the counter and greeted her with my usual "Good day, Patou, how's it going?" But it was only after the words left my mouth that I realized I wasn't speaking French.

"I am fine, Ira," Patou replied with a lilting accent. "And how is it going for you?"

I was stunned. "You speak English?"

"Yes. We are taught in school."

"Then why did you let me stumble through my awful French?"

"Because you were trying so hard, and to answer you in English would have been impolite."

I appreciated Patou's consideration for my feelings. This starkly contrasted with the waiters at bustling Parisian cafés who routinely answered my French in English. But here in polite Provence, there apparently was a rule that a conversation initiated in French required a response in French.

I now wondered if this rule extended to English. "Patou," I asked, "what if I walked into another store in town and began with 'Hello, how are you?' If the proprietor responded in English, we'd get on with life. Otherwise, I'd simply lapse back into fractured French."

Patou admonished me with a wave of her forefinger. "Ira, when you are in France, you should speak

French." She went on to explain that although many shopkeepers knew some English, their opportunity to hear and speak it was limited to the summer season. Therefore, if I tried to force people to speak English when they weren't comfortable, it would also be impolite.

Patou knew I wasn't going to become fluent in French overnight, so she suggested that after the French greetings, I simply ask the shopkeeper, "Do you speak English?" She added that I might not be successful at the businesses that serve residents, such as Le Petit Casino and the farmer's market, but switching to English should work at places frequented by tourists, such as the hotels, restaurants and cafés.

I was learning a lot from Patou. Over time, as our friendship evolved, Patou introduced me to her brother, Daniel, and later to their parents. The family owned other businesses—a gift shop and a fine Provençal restaurant—and Barbara and I were warmly welcomed whenever we stopped by. And if they saw us driving our lime-green Peugeot in town, Patou and her family would always wave and smile.

Our world had been enriched. We were no longer only in the company of doves, squirrels and wild boar. We were no longer isolated from the community in which we lived. We had developed a warm and enduring friendship with a local family, and it changed the way we viewed La Chandelle and the South of France: the villa was no longer just a charming and peaceful vacation spot; it began to feel like our second home.

Spandex-By-The-Sea

"THE MAN WHO INVENTED Spandex sits at the right-hand-side of God," my husband remarked as he watched a seemingly endless parade of shapely, long-legged women walking along the quai Suffren. Only the colors of their clothing made it possible to tell where skin ended and material began.

Having settled in at La Chandelle, this was our first trip to St-Tropez for the season, and we had taken a front row table at the Café de Paris to watch the portside spectacle. Although I had read somewhere that café patrons were considered "in" only if they sat in the back, it would have required divine intervention to dislodge Ira from his ringside seat.

"I wonder if there's something in the air that makes these women so tall and long-legged," my husband mused, "or whether the world's tall, long-legged women simply gravitate here."

"Brigitte Bardot's movie, *And God Created Woman*, probably set the tone," I said. "Since then, St-Tropez has evolved into the sex symbol of the South of France, the pinnacle of chic, the playground of . . . " I was distracted by a sudden buzz of activity on the afterdeck of a $50,000,000 yacht that was moored directly in front of us. Now it was *I* who was in heaven as I watched gorgeous crewmembers, tanned and impeccably dressed in white uniforms, prepare for the arrival of the ship's dinner guests. From the crew's dark good looks I conjectured that these young men were from Italy to the east or Spain to the west.

I followed their every move as they positioned exquisite furniture, covered the dining table with linens, executed precise place settings of china, silver, and crystal, and added a spectacular arrangement of cut, fresh flowers to the center of the table. I then noticed that this centerpiece ceremony was simultaneously occurring on neighboring super yachts, with each crew seeming to compete with the other for floral artistry and scale.

Having completed their work, the young men in front of us relaxed and talked among themselves, and occasionally with passers-by, as they waited for the guests to arrive. Behind them the doors remained open, revealing salons as large and as graciously decorated as those in the most exquisite of homes.

As we finished our wine, I noticed activity at the Sénéquier, a café to our right. Some of the patrons had left their tables and were heading toward the boarding ramps. The men wore sport jackets, shirts opened at the collar; the women carried designer bags, their jewelry flashing in the sun. I later learned that Sénéquier was considered *the* café at the old port, and if you sat at its front, sooner or later everyone in the world would pass you by.

Ever since Ira had stumbled upon this incredible scene last fall, I had been looking forward to returning to St-Tropez. Earlier in the day, while I was getting ready for our first night out on the town, I had willed the weather to be absolutely perfect. And it was. We had departed Ste-Maxime at 6 p.m., and were rewarded by a clear blue sky over an aquamarine sea, with coastal towns and white sand beaches awash in the sun's golden glow.

After twenty minutes on a tree-shaded highway, we had reached the city limits and a fork in the road. Place de Lices, the town plaza, was to our right, and the massive Parking du Port to our left. We chose the port, parked the Peugeot, and as we walked past the last row of cars we were treated to a montage of pastel buildings, yachts, sidewalk cafés, and street artists, all highlighted by the sun.

Since our visit last September, I had studied the map of this area and learned that the *vieux port* was part of a small peninsula that curved back toward Ste-Maxime, clearly visible across the waters of the Golfe of St-Tropez. Whereas most of France's other Mediterranean towns had a southerly orientation, St-Tropez, like many coastal cities in California, faced northwest and into the sun. The direct light on the frescoed buildings fronting the water turned amber in early evening, and it was easy to see why this vista was a favorite of the street artists. But it was also this westerly exposure that could make sitting in a front row table at the Café de Paris uncomfortable, and after an hour of ogling we began to melt. Since it was still too early for the restaurants to open, we decided to make the Café des Arts, another subject favored by street artists, our next stop.

Ira, looking at a street map that he had picked up at the tourist bureau at the port, determined that Rue Georges Clemenceau would take us directly to the plaza. But neither of us had anticipated that the street would be lined with trendy shops selling everything from elegant home furnishings to designer clothing. I had seen such stores in the swank sections of Paris and Rome, but I never expected to find Hermes and Calvin Klein in a small town in Provence.

"*Voilà!*" Ira pointed, attempting to save himself from my sudden enthusiasm for window-shopping. He took my arm and guided me into the Place des Lices. But upscale shops surrounded the square as well, so the tug-of-war continued until I found myself planted in the middle of a traditional Provençal plaza. Around me were various groups of men intently focused on the game of *boules*. No Spandex here—rather brown leather shoes, heavy black cotton trousers, white sleeveless undershirts, suspenders. An occasional younger man, an occasional woman, but predominantly gray-haired, wiry men who concentrated on rolling a large *boule* as close to a small *cochonnet* as possible. Generally quiet, players only erupted when a shot landed near the target, or knocked an opponent's *boule* out of contention.

We found the Café des Arts in a corner of the square and chose a table in filtered sunlight. Slowly sipping our wine, we watched as working people from the neighborhood, some with their children and dogs, walked in, greeted one another, and sat around talking, smoking, and drinking.

Lacking the diversions of the port, Ira began thumbing through our guidebook, curious as to why this particular café had been singled out by the street artists. "Now it makes sense," he said. "This is an historic place, the spot where famous post-Impressionistic painters and intellectuals from Paris have gathered for years. Even BB and her 'glam' friends have hung out here." Ira quickly glanced around. Not seeing Bardot, he returned to his reading. Then he did a double take. "Wait a minute. Something's wrong." He tapped on an illustration and turned the book toward me.

"What am I looking at?"

"The caption says this is a 1925 painting of the Café des Arts by Charles Camoin, a disciple of the artist Paul Signac. But the drawing isn't of *this* establishment: It depicts a place now called Le Café." My husband motioned to his right. "It's over there, just a few doors down."

I glanced in the direction my husband was pointing, but any curiosity I had regarding the two Café des Arts was quickly replaced with another curiosity: "Where are we going to eat tonight? I'm starving."

"How about Mexican?" Ira offered.

"What?"

"Mexican. It says in here that 'El Mexicano is one of the best kept secrets of St-Tropez.'"

"Maybe it should stay that way."

"It's a neighborhood place in the *quartier de la Ponche,* the town's old fishing harbor. It's not a tourist spot, so we can see what the French *really* eat."

"Tacos? Chile con carne? I don't think so."

"Think of Mexican dishes prepared with a French twist. Moreover, we'll recognize the menu. If we go to a French restaurant without having done our homework, we might wind up with a local delicacy that's trying to wiggle away from our forks. Besides, El Mexicano is only a short walk from here."

"Okay," I relented. It was 8 p.m., and I was too hungry to argue.

We paid *l'addition* and Ira took my hand, leading me out of the plaza and down Rue Gambetta, another upscale shopping street. But this time I walked with deliberation, foregoing window-shopping for food. We suddenly turned right, passing through the arches of the seventeenth-century Chappelle de la Miséricorde and onto a passageway. More turns and several narrow streets later, Ira stopped to look at the map.

"You're lost, aren't you?" I was making no effort to hide the irritation in my voice.

"Don't worry," he said, pointing to a steeple rising above the roofline. That's the Église de St-Tropez; our Mexican restaurant is only a short walk from there."

I had my hands on my hips. "I thought *your* Mexican restaurant was 'only a short walk' from the plaza."

"Don't worry. I know where I'm going."

"Ha!" I said.

Five minutes later we were in front of the *église*. While Ira was studying the map, I was studying the church in an attempt to take my mind off food. The main structure was painted in traditional Provençal terra cotta, crowned by a yellow campanile and a wrought iron bell tower. I opened the church's large wooden doors. Maybe there was food inside. Ira took my arm. I took a church pamphlet.

"The restaurant's this way," he said.

"Ha!"

After weaving our way through a maze of small streets, after passing dozens of restaurants packed with tourists happily devouring gourmet meals, after enduring the aroma of fine French food wafting from a hundred kitchens, we finally arrived in the *quartier de la Ponche*. We found El Mexicano easily enough, but the place was completely empty—there were no patrons seated outside, nor were there any inside.

Ira read my mind. "It only confirms that this *is* a local haunt. The French don't eat this early."

"Ha!"

By now I was too weak to seek out another restaurant and wait to be seated, so we took a table outside. As dusk settled over St-Tropez, we sipped Margaritas, followed by one of the finest interpretations of Mexican cuisine either of us had ever experienced. At nine o'clock, the noise level rose as the restaurant began to fill with music, laughter, and neighborhood people who knew the proprietors well.

Near the end of dinner, I brought the conversation back to the *église*. "I'd like to attend mass one of these Sundays. The inside is tastefully ornate."

"Uh-huh," Ira said, dipping a bite of salmon in a delicate lime-cilantro sauce.

"I understand the congregation sings the service."

"Uh-huh," Ira said, through a mouthful of cornbread.

He had a "life is good" look on his face, meaning I could commit him to something he would normally not do—like going to church while on vacation.

"Mass begins at 10:30 on Sunday morning. We can easily make that, don't you think?"

"Uh-huh," Ira said.

I wanted Ira's attention. "The *église* has the head of Saint Torpes, the patron saint of St-Tropez, on display," I said, casually reading from the church's pamphlet.

"Really? His actual head?"

"No, it's a replica. It goes on to say that Torpes was a high-level Roman soldier in Nero's army who was beheaded for converting to Christianity. His decapitated body was then set adrift in a boat, along with a dog and a cockerel. The Romans figured the animals would devour him, but the miracle is that the boat landed here in AD 68 with the saint's headless body completely intact."

"If they wound up with just the body, why don't they put *it* on display?"

"Beats me."

"It makes no sense."

"There's more: 'Each year, on May 16, the town celebrates Saint Torpes' day with a festival called *Les Bravades*. The town captain, carrying the saint's head, marches through the streets, leading an army of flag-waving, blunderbuss-firing *bravadeurs* who are dressed in French revolutionary uniforms. The procession winds up at the sea which is blessed for safely delivering the headless body to St-Tropez' shores.'"

"What do guns and the French Revolution have to do with a beheaded Roman soldier? What's the connection?"

I shrugged. "I don't know."

"It still makes no sense. A *faux* Café des Arts. A French Mexican restaurant. A bizarre *bravade*. This place is weird—I like it."

We finished our meal. Dusk had now edged into night and we decided to have coffee back at the port. We chose the second floor lounge at the Hôtel Sube, which gave us a bird's eye view of the action below. The hotel was located next to the Café de Paris, where we had started out three hours earlier. The symmetry of the evening appealed to us.

The hotel's entrance was located behind a statue of Admiral Pierre Andre de Suffren. A plaque identified him as the "Terror of the English" because he and his crew of Tropéziens had thwarted a British naval attack in the eighteenth century. We entered the small and charming hotel and climbed to the second floor where paned glass doors opened onto a balcony overlooking the port. We sat at a table and ordered cappuccinos. Below us was a steady stream of people promenading along the quay. At intervals stood mimes in gold and silver paint. Nearby, the paparazzi, hair tied back in ponytails, looked this way and that, hoping for a photo of Naomi Campbell, Robert De Niro, Jack Nicholson, or one of the other stars who might be in town for dinner. Beyond the crowd, on the afterdecks of the floating gin palaces, the men smoked cigars and sipped brandy, watching the spectators watching them.

Meanwhile, in the bar behind us, several casually chic twenty-to-thirty-year-olds lounged in overstuffed couches and chairs, under walls filled with photos of the successors to Admiral Suffren, modern-day sailors racing magnificent vessels, sails and spinnakers billowing, the America's Cup their goal. The young French patrons were engaged in a blur of conversations, more interested in one another than in the unfinished drinks in front of them.

Ira signaled and the waitress arrived with the bill. "These are expensive cups of coffee," I remarked.

"We're buying more than coffee," Ira replied. "If you've noticed, once customers order anything, even a bottle of mineral water, they're free to remain here, or at the sidewalk cafés—anywhere—for as long as they wish."

As we sat staring at the moon, its light casting a silvery glow over the Mediterranean, I added, "So we're not just buying a drink; we're leasing space at some of the most beautiful real estate in the world."

The Poop on the Pissoir

IN THE EXCITEMENT of leasing real estate overlooking the Mediterranean, I neglected to lease a few moments in the Hôtel Sube's restroom. Ira and I were hiking back to our Peugeot in the port's mammoth parking lot, so I drew to an abrupt halt when we happened upon a large, automated *toilette*.

I understood that one finds comfort in tending to bodily functions within the privacy of one's own bathroom and behind closed doors. In gender-separated public restrooms, the anonymity of multiple stalls helped to create some of that same sense of privacy.

I also understood that such comfort was lost with the single, unisex toilet located, for example, in a commercial airliner. Long lines of passengers-in-waiting monitor the comings and goings of each patron, who experiences a sense of accomplishment when she is the recipient of appreciative smiles, a reward for expediency. Icy stares punish those who are dilatory with the hope that these transgressors will slink back to their seats, to stay, for the remainder of the flight.

It was within this context of potential public humiliation that I contemplated my first intimate experience with the automated French toilet. My female friends and I had discussed these French auto-potties, shiploads of which had now infiltrated the United States. We had all read about their cleanliness—how they were completely sanitized after each use.

But we had questions: Did they actually work? Was the interior sprayed, only to leave a wet toilet seat in its wake? Was a chemical used? Wet toilet seats replaced by possible asphyxiation?

And what about privacy? Those motorized monoliths were positioned in public places where perfect strangers could walk by, queue up, and surround us as we did our thing.

But could the French be wrong?

Questions of such significance should be entrusted only to the most dependable of individuals. And so I did what any logical woman would do. I asked my husband to try it first and tell me all about it.

We approached the tall silver structure, roughly cylindrical in shape, and determined we had the requisite eurocents. Circling our target, we estimated it stood seven feet high and eight feet in circumference. As we worked our way around to the front, a light on the door abruptly halted our inspection. It declared that the unit was *OCCUPÉ*, a surprising fact considering that we had encountered no other people in this large lot.

But, after all, this *was* St-Tropez, one of the sexiest places on Earth, and we conjectured that the loo—for the bargain price of fifty cents—could easily be used *par deux*.

Ira and I moved on and we found another obelisk. This time its status light announced *LIBRE*. By now my own needs forced me to throw caution to the wind. I readied my *monnaie* and posed while Ira took my picture, a memorial, I nervously joked, about never returning.

The door had no handle but opened automatically after I inserted my coins. Once I was inside, it slid shut, entombing me in a large, dimly lit, silver casket. There was a slight chemical odor to the air.

I quickly considered my means of escape. There were two—*if* everything worked properly: an internal handle that theoretically activated the door manually; or, at the expiration of my allotted time, the door was to open automatically.

Unfortunately, I had no clue as to what my allotted time might be. What if the door opened while I was seated on the toilet? From that position I could not reach the handle to fight it shut. And if I left my seat momentarily, would that initiate the automatic cleaning function?

I remembered reading a warning that children should not be allowed to use these robotic restrooms without adult supervision because of the danger of being trapped inside during the cleaning cycle. I imagined myself exposed, sitting in *exactly* the wrong place, when a torrent of disinfectant was unleashed upon my person.

For a moment these thoughts paralyzed me, and I debated whether or not I really wanted to go through with this experience. But I also knew my hesitancy was using up my allotted time, so I compromised by proceeding as expeditiously as possible, ever ready to pounce in the event of an errantly automated door.

When that portion of my experience was behind me, I noticed there were no faucets, sinks or towels. Instead, a sign directed me to insert my hands into a rectangular enclosure where I presumed they were to be sanitized by the eerie purple light. That being done, and with a quick glance around, I decided to make my exit.

But then came a moment of barely controlled panic when I could not figure out how to open the door. I jerked the handle several times. I became more frantic by the second. Suddenly the door receded and, feeling immense relief, I quickly stepped into the cool night air, the darkness masking the panicked look of an escapee on my face.

Standing a short distance away, a young couple giggled as they searched each other's pockets for fifty eurocents. Behind me the door slid closed, and the light flashed *OCCUPÉ*. I imagined a showering spray of disinfectant and a flowing purple presence that hid themselves once the light again read *LIBRE,* allowing the couple-in-waiting to insert their coins and step inside.

--- ---→

There had been a time, some years ago, when a French auto-potty would have been a welcome sight. I had arrived in Paris for my first visit. The City of Lights. The Louvre, Notre Dame, the Sorbonne. I was ready to see them all, to fill myself with the history, the culture, the elegance.

But first I needed to go to the bathroom.

I knew from my guidebook that men and women generally used the same lavatories in Europe, and I was fully prepared to experience *la toilette* unisex. I was not prepared, however, to open a door into pitch-blackness.

Stifling the urge to turn and leave, in part because I was now a world traveler, and in part because I had to go, I ran my hand up and down the walls until I located the light switch with which I illuminated, to my horror, a few feet in front of me, a hole in the ground. From the two tiled foot forms on the right and left sides of a gaping aperture, I assumed that I was intended to stand or squat over the cavern and do my business.

The architect of this travesty could only have been a man.

Think of the French couture, of Hermes, of Chanel, of Cardin. Think of skirts, tights, and undergarments. Think of how I really wanted to exit what could only be called a hellhole. But for what? Would all of France be the same? I could only assume yes.

But with time of the essence, with mobility constrained by clothing, and with all the courage I could muster, I cautiously positioned my left foot into the form and . . . the lights suddenly went out.

Was there a switch in the footprint? Did French civility prohibit use of this most arcane of toilets except in total darkness?

I stepped backward. Carefully.

Once again groping, I located the wall switch and turned on the lights. I returned to the left form and waited for a moment.

The lights stayed on.

I stepped into the right form. I was about to begin when I was once again plunged into total darkness. But now, under the pressure of nature, and with all the dexterity I could muster, I did what I had to do, in the dark, and left.

I later learned I had been initiated into the ranks of worldly women by an ancient Turkish toilet with an energy conserving twist—a timer-controlled light switch. So it was with great relief when I entered my first Parisian hotel room and thought myself blessed. *Two pissoirs in the bathroom?* I thought. *Curious, but luxurious.*

Upon closer examination I noticed that the two *toilettes* were configured differently. One could be flushed, but the other simply had a drain and looked like a little, elevated bathtub. Since I only needed one toilet, I decided to put the other to good use as the perfect place in which to wash clothes, a practice I continued as I traveled throughout Europe. Even after I learned about bidets.

The bidet, when used as intended, reveals much about French attitudes toward hygiene and sex. But what did the holes in the ground suggest?

I did not even want to know.

Instead I reflected on the contradictions I had experienced, and on the bathroom in the Casino at Monte Carlo where I would take visiting women friends past the roulette wheel and the baccarat table, directing them instead to the Casino's legendary women's lounge.

Upon entering *le grand salon de la toilette*, my friend was immediately impressed by the attention to detail: the Italian marble, the inlaid gold, and the ornate mirrors.

But it was only when she opened the door to the stall itself did she experience one of the technological marvels of the world—*La Toilette*. Sensing the presence of a guest, it comes alive, lowers its seat, and then covers itself with sterilized paper.

After the guest stands, the toilet automatically removes its paper cover, flushes, and raises its seat, all in preparation for the next visitor.

The architect of *La Toilette*. She is definitely a woman.

Cavaillon Melons

WE WERE LYING on the beach in Nice. Ira was reading. I was pondering life's imponderables. Looking about me, I reflected that there came a point in life when we first learned about the French Riviera. Featured in this newly acquired knowledge were the B-words: breasts, beaches, and—depending on one's age—Brigitte Bardot. Among these subjects, breasts seem to stand out. And depending on one's gender, one might either be excited or intimidated by a culture that fosters semi-naked women on public display.

One of the rewarding aspects of a long-term and honest relationship with a member of the opposite sex is the ability to find stuff out. It was like capturing a spy from the other camp. But instead of torture, the security of my relationship and the simple passage of time allowed me to learn things from my spouse I normally would never know. It was in this context that I rolled onto my side and asked Ira, "What did the Riviera bring to mind before you actually came here?"

"Breasts. And long hair, long legs, bronzed bodies, sandy beaches, and me—perfectly free to check it all out. I was a teenager at the time, and when I heard about *the* Riviera, it was my idea of heaven, along with *Playboy* magazine. What about you?"

"Well," I hesitated. "I wasn't a prude as a teenager. And I didn't object to the French custom of going topless—even though in America the proper standard for beachwear has always been much more conservative. It seemed to take forever to evolve

81

from the maillot to the two-piece bathing suit and, finally, to the bikini.

"Although I thought people could do whatever they wanted, I personally had a problem with going topless. I imagined myself on the Riviera some day, and I wondered what I'd do. Would I be so bold as to discard my top and expose two bright white breasts? Or would I be too embarrassed, and suffer the discomfort of being considered old-fashioned by other beachgoers or, even worse, by my free-spirited traveling companions who might just throw caution and swimsuit tops to the wind? Either way it gave me angst just thinking about it."

"Don't you think we both focused too much on breasts?"

"Maybe. Here we are in the land of Monet, Picasso, Cézanne. Here we are in the land of authors, vintners, and gourmands, the land where art, culture, and haute cuisine dominate the focus of the people— not breasts.

Even when surrounded by beautifully tanned female bodies, the Frenchman does not stare. He displays, at most, a casual interest. But an American male will dart his head around as if he were trying to follow a moth on methamphetamine."

"That's probably an overstatement," Ira said.

"Right. And what did your buddies want to know when you got back from your first trip to France?"

"Did you visit a topless beach?"

"And the second question?"

"Got any pictures?"

I sat upright and threw my nose up in the air. "But now that we're worldly travelers, we dismiss such voyeuristic questions with a wave of the hand."

"Maybe," Ira said. "But I remember the first time I arrived in Nice with my fantasies intact. I remember being in the back of a taxi as it sped down the Promenade Des Anglais, the Mediterranean to my right, and me straining, unsuccessfully, to get a glimpse of some topless girls."

"For different reasons, I did the same thing."

"I remember stepping onto the beach in baggy surfer shorts . . ."

"I had on an attractive, but modest, bikini."

". . . and I saw it was not really a beach at all, but a narrow band of rocks and pebbles. Children ran around completely naked, while the English and German matrons covered themselves in one-piece suits."

"Yes, and their elderly husbands uniformly wore tiny black nylon trunks that bulged in every direction beneath oversized bellies."

"Right," my husband agreed. "But the French women were something else. They seemed comfortable with their bodies, exposing breasts that were huge, small, wrinkled, smooth, sagging, firm." Ira's eyes scanned the beach. "And," he continued, "sprinkled among those children, parents, and grandparents were the topless, long-legged beauties whose photographs appeared on the postcards I sent home to my buddies with the inscription, 'Having a wonderful time.'"

"So do you feel any differently now?" I asked.

"Sure. I don't dart my head around like I was following a moth on methamphetamine."

"No, I'm serious," I said.

"So am I. Initially what I saw created tremendous visual stimulation for me. I mean I was never so uncool that I walked around on the beach with a camera or a video recorder, semi-surreptitiously shooting topless women like some other men I've seen.

"It's taken years, but now as I sit on the beach surrounded by the subjects of my earlier postcards, I may read, I may glance up to appreciate a beautiful body, I may be entertained, but I feel more like I think a Frenchman must feel. You're not a pervert staring at topless women. You're lost in the scene, not self-conscious."

"Well for me," I said, "I've seen such an array of body types that I'm not as judgmental as I used to be. Breasts, legs, arms . . . everything seems to blend and nothing specific gets my attention—with one exception."

"What's that?" Ira asked.

"Cavaillon melons."

"I don't understand."

"Somebody once told me you can tell when a woman had implants because each breast was round, and always maintained its shape, even if she was lying on her back when most women's breasts, no matter what size, tend to flatten and spread out. But at home I don't have an array of naked women giving me exemplars from which I could be educated.

"Then the other day I noticed this young woman on the beach, topless, and each of her breasts was perfectly round. And I realized that they looked like they were stuffed with Cavaillon melons. That created such a silly image in my mind that I can't ignore it whenever a pair of Cavaillons goes by. I guess I'll need more time so that I can become as suave and sophisticated as you."

"Never happen. But you did remind me of something else. We always joke about how wonderful it is that so many 'fathers' bring their voluptuous 'daughters' on vacations, and how nice it is that these 'fathers' take their 'daughters' shopping in designer stores and then take them to expensive restaurants."

"Right," I said. "It's those same 'fathers' who escort their topless 'daughters' to the beach and help them select thongs at the swimsuit boutiques."

"I remember seeing three of these 'father-and-daughter' couples the other night," Ira said. "They got my attention because they were lined up for a picture. And each of the 'daughters' wore a low-necked gown. Now as I look back on that scene I realize I was seeing—"

"—let me guess," I said. "Cavaillon melons?"

The Starry Night

STRONG BREEZE had been blowing when Ira and I went to bed. Nothing unusual. But in the morning when I opened the shutters I saw our lawn furniture—tables, chairs, umbrellas—floating in the pool. Lounge mats were splayed haphazardly on the hillside; rafts and pool toys were lodged in the *pin parasols.* My mind imagined our vinyl turtles and frogs, wide-eyed as they sailed helplessly through the black night, their short appendages flailing as the wind heaved them against tree trunks or impaled them on branches. For, while we were peacefully sleeping within the protection of our villa, all things outside those walls had been subjected to the ravages of—our first mistral.

I had always assumed the winds had been named for Frederic Mistral, the Nobel laureate who had lived in this area in the late 1800s and for whom the street leading to the Église de St-Tropez was named. Wrong. The wind was not even indigenous to this part of the world. Instead, getting its name from *mistrau,* or master, it originates 1,000 miles north in Siberia, picks up speed as it roars down France's Rhone Valley, turns left, and slams into Provence.

For the earlier settlers of this region, whose knowledge of geography did not extend to Siberia, the source of the evil mistral was Mont Ventoux, the huge humpbacked massif forming the northern boundary of Provence. The Celts believed Mont Ventoux was the Home of the Winds, a holy place. And the medieval Christians, to whom the massif's cold gusts were evil, attempted to exorcise the wind in chapels they built along its slopes.

The mistral was able to drop the temperature by twenty degrees instantly, have wind gusts to 180 km per hour, and last for several days. It had become the custom of the French to blame it for driving people mad and, in fact, an old law in Provence acquitted a murderer if he could prove his victim was killed while the mistral was blowing.

Ira wondered out loud if this would be his fate when our landlord learned that his crystalline pool, his pride and joy, the centerpiece of La Chandelle, had been turned into a tureen of pea soup by the mistral. My husband was shaking his head as he pulled the last lawn chair from the green water. "Monsieur Martignon is going to kill me," he kept saying.

"Why? Just add some salt," I said.

Ira kept shaking his head. "I'm not going to taste the pool water any more. I refuse. Besides, it's going to take a lot more than salt to fix this mess."

"What do we have to do?"

"I have no idea. But I told you we shouldn't have cranked up the temperature of the pool. The wind has been blowing organic matter into the warm water, causing the level of bacteria to increase, which in turn is causing the water temperature to rise, which in turn is causing the bacteria to multiply, which in turn is boosting the temperature. Look at the pool thermometer: it's already 33 degrees centigrade and climbing. Soon we'll have a bubbling, green caldron. Monsieur Martignon, he's definitely going to kill me."

For the next few hours, my husband obsessively skimmed the pool, hoisting debris with a net at the end of a ten-foot pole. But it was a losing battle as strong gusts periodically swept down from the sky and copious amounts of pine needles from our *pin parasol* trees would rain into the water. Just as it had been foretold by French folklore, my husband had clearly succumbed to the madness of the mistral. I feared that the next net in the scene would be a much larger one. For him.

His shoulders sagged in defeat as I approached. "It's time to phone Monsieur," I said in my most soothing tone.

Ira sighed, went into the villa, and picked up the telephone. After the customary pleasantries, he explained the situation: "Monsieur Martignon, we are having a mistral. The pool has turned green. The frogs living in the neighbor's pond across the street are descending upon us like tourists on the Riviera."

With images of French frogs carrying pool floats of lily pads marching up the hillside to vacation in the warm, green waters of our pool, I was hoping that Ira's attempt to duplicate Monsieur's droll humor would prove successful.

After a few moments my husband cradled the phone and turned to me. "He's concerned, so he's going to drive up later today."

While I would never admit it to Ira, I was afraid my insistence on warmer water actually did trigger this whole mess, and that I had ruined an expensive, computerized pool system. My punishment would be an uninhabitable green swamp for the remaining weeks of our vacation, a hefty repair bill, plus an invitation from the landlord to remain in America.

When Monsieur Martignon arrived, I hid in the house. Even though Ira had turned the pool's heating system off, I was certain the green stagnant water would reveal what I had done.

"He's gone," my husband said, finding me in bed and under the covers, with windows and draperies closed.

I sat up. "Did he fix it?"

"Probably. He added some chlorine and more salt, telling me to do the same for the next three days. By then the pool should be back to normal."

"Was he angry?"

"I don't think so. Before he left he gave me this recipe for frog's legs," Ira said, holding up a slip of paper. "The secret is a quick dusting with seasoned flour before sautéing in butter."

"Did he figure out we had raised the temperature of the pool?"

"It didn't come up. But I confessed because his heating bill is going to be much larger than normal, which is probably around zero this time of year. I told him we would pay it. I also said we would rely on the sun to warm the pool from now on."

The next day broke fresh and clear, with only an occasional strong breeze to remind me of yesterday's storm. Although mistrals nearly always last for three days, they can be much shorter when they begin at night, as this one had. The air was warm, so I slipped into my bathing suit and stood at the edge of our pool. The water was a lighter shade of green, and I could begin to make out the small, blue tile squares that lined the bottom.

Ira didn't want me swimming just yet, so I climbed onto a raft and let the breeze blow me gently across the pool. I gazed over the lawn at our villa. Now it made sense. It was constructed consistently with the *mas,* the stucco and tile farmhouses of Provence, which are protected from the northwest wind with a southeast orientation and low roofline. Our villa's rear windows, facing the wind, were small and barred, while those in front opened expansively onto the grounds, pool, and the sea beyond.

By evening, the wind had completely died down and we took our dinner on the patio. "There are some good things about the mistral," I said. "It cleans the air of haze and allows for that golden light we love so much."

"And the clear night air too," Ira said.

We leaned back in our chairs, looking at the bright, twinkling lights filling the evening sky.

The magic of the mistral had transported us into Vincent Van Gogh's *The Starry Night,* one of his last paintings done while he was a patient in the asylum at Saint-Rémy. He had rendered the night sky in rolling waves, as if the mistral were sweeping his strokes across the canvas, exaggerating the size and brightness of the moon and stars. At the time he said, "Looking at the stars always makes me dream . . . just as we take the train to get to Tarascon or Rouen, we take death to reach a star." His words had always stuck with me.

Not long after painting *The Starry Night,* Van Gogh committed suicide. He had struggled with mental illness. Some say he was drinking too much absinthe, a potent liqueur that was thought to stimulate creativity. Others say it was epilepsy.

I shared these thoughts with Ira. "But I have a different theory," I said.

"What's that?"

"It was the mistral."

Bzzzzzzzz

Bzzzzzzzzz.
 I was awake. But if I didn't move and didn't hear anything, it didn't exist.

Bzzzzzzzzz.

I looked over at Ira. He was sound asleep. Well there was no way I was going to be able to deal with this mosquito without lights. I turned on my bedside lamp. I looked over at Ira. He was still sound asleep. I got up and turned on the overhead lights and stood perfectly still. My mind and unblinking eyes focused, surveillance cameras scouring the room for The Mosquito. Minutes passed. Nothing. I relaxed, turned and moved toward the light switch.

Bzzzzzzzzz.

I swung back around. There it was. Partially obscured by the ruffled valance that topped Madame's canopy bed. They always liked to hide there. Almost perfect camouflage. But not this time. I picked up a sock that Ira had left on the floor. I swung. I missed.

The Mosquito retreated to the other side of the bed. I could not tell if it was wounded. I looked down at Ira. He was still asleep. The Mosquito and I were not. It moved to the highest point of the four-poster bed and out of my reach. I hurled the sock at it. I missed. The Mosquito. I hit Ira. He bolted straight up. "What are you doing?"

"Trying to kill a mosquito that has been keeping *me* awake."

"Use the bug spray."

"But if I use the bug spray, the room will smell of chemicals all night."

93

"You can leave the window open," Ira said.

"Then more mosquitoes will come in."

Ira looked at me.

I got the bug spray and returned to the bedroom. This time my husband and I both assumed the roles of sentries. Silence. Then Ira shouted, "I see him. He's over here."

I ran to Ira's side of the bed and sprayed. I missed. The Mosquito. I hit Ira. "What do you think you're doing?" Ira grabbed the can and sprayed at The Mosquito. Its bunker saturated, The Mosquito flew down the hallway, followed by a wild man, canister raised above his head, bug spray in his wake.

I waited in the bedroom. Ira returned. "I got him."

We compromised on leaving the window open just a bit, turned off the lights, and returned to bed. My exhaustion tranquilized me into accepting my husband's opinion that the bug spray in our bedroom was not harmful. As for the odor, I figured I would not smell that when I was asleep. I closed my eyes and, whether by asphyxiation or by nature, began to drift off.

Bzzzzzzzzz.

Over coffee the following morning, we conducted our debriefing. Ira began. "You know, the temperature is so perfect around here this time of year, we hardly ever have a problem with mosquitoes. During the night, it's usually in the low sixties, we leave the windows closed, and we're perfectly comfortable inside. If you think it's important to deal with those few hot evenings which are an exception, maybe we could talk to Monsieur or one of the people we've met around here, and get their opinion of what we should do."

"I have all the opinions I need," I said. "Me, myself and I. And I want to be able to keep the windows open *and* not have mosquitoes. These places should have screens."

"We've never seen a villa around here with screens," Ira said. "But the irony is that the French seem obsessed with mosquitoes. They have billboards along major roads that each year announce the actual date of the mosquitoes' arrival. They have sprays to kill them. They have torches, candles, and incense to keep them at a distance. But the French shun screens because they like to look out their windows with nothing between them and the outdoors. They love their surroundings and don't want to screen themselves in. You know how one of your favorite things is to wake up in the morning, open the shutters and your arms to welcome the air and light that is the beauty of a Provençal morning. Nothing separating you and nature.

"And you know how I love to reach out onto the window ledge," Ira continued, "and pick fresh basil for our salads from the potted plant we have growing there."

"I want to go to that hardware and garden supply store we saw near St-Tropez and see what we can find," I said.

"Perhaps *Madame* would care to try a *ventilateur?*"

"Tell him *Madame* would not like to try a fan. Tell him that *Madame* wishes a natural environment, not one filled with *le petit faux mistral.*"

Ira looked at the clerk and, as was becoming his custom, raised his palms and shrugged. The two of them quietly conferred, and I then followed as we were guided through the store, stopping on occasion to discuss some item pulled from the shelf. We left the *jardinière* with an insect repellent device, which is what, the clerk had explained, the French used to combat mosquitoes and which I had dubiously agreed to try—plus the materials necessary to screen in our bedroom windows—which is what I knew we would really need.

The following day, my husband called me over to see his handiwork. While I did not know exactly what to expect, I did not anticipate screening taped to frames of anorexic bamboo inserted into, but not at-tached to, the recessed walls surrounding the win-dows. I debated as to whether I should show appre-ciation or honest skepticism and defaulted to silence. Guaranteeing that his screen design would work, Ira went into the house.

That night we fell asleep peacefully, with a soft breeze from the open, screened window.

Bzzzzzzzzz.

I was wide-awake. "Ira—I thought I had a guar-antee."

"There is no way a mosquito could get through that screening," Ira said.

Bzzzzzzzzz.

"And what I hear is . . . ?" I stared at my hus-band.

"Here's what I'll do," he said. "I'll open up the bedroom, herd the mosquito outside, and shut the door behind it." Even as he spoke, my husband was unlatching the shutter, opening the door to our room, and flailing his arms at our uninvited guest. But flail as he would, the mosquito seemed to have established a permanent orbit around my husband's head.

"Okay. I'm going to go outside; he'll come with me; I'll run back in and, *voilà*, no more mosquito." Ira went out; the mosquito went out. Ira came in; the mosquito came in.

"Where is that electronic gizmo we bought?" I asked. My patience, but not the mosquito's, had expired.

I pulled what looked like one-half of a red tennis ball from the drawer to which Ira had pointed. The gadget's flattened backside had prongs designed for a French electrical outlet. I returned to our bedroom and inserted it into the floor-level socket.

"Do you think the mosquitoes line up and just march to this thing where they are electrocuted?" I asked. "So what do you think will keep us awake now? Their screams? Maybe the funeral dirge hummed in the key of bzzzzzz minor by survivors for their fallen colleagues?

"Or maybe, waking up in the middle of the night and walking to the bathroom, we bump into the thing, are electrocuted, and won't have to worry about mosquitoes anymore."

"I think you're supposed to put something in it." Ira was reading the instructions.

I went back to the table where he had laid out the rest of our purchases. The boxes identified the gizmo as a *Diffuseur Electrique* and promised "*nuits sans moustiques même fenêtres ouvertes.*"   Well, that's what I wanted—nights without mosquitoes and the windows open. I picked up a box that held dozens of rectangular-shaped objects individually secured in foil, tore one open, pulled out a blue rectangle, and walked back into the bedroom. I reached for the tennis ball.

"*Merde!*"

As Ira came running in, the ball was flying into the air, and I was massaging my right hand. "I figured it out. This thing burns you so badly that a mosquito bite seems preferable in comparison. It's humans, not mosquitoes, who are supposed to queue up for electrocution."

By the time my speech was over, the thing had cooled down enough for Ira to pick it up. He walked back to the dining room table. I followed. At a distance.

"It seems like there is a place to slide these little blue wafers behind the grating at the front." Doing that, Ira then returned to the bedroom and reinserted the thing into the outlet. We stared. Nothing happened. To us. We didn't know about the mosquitoes.

After we thought it was safe to do so, we climbed into bed.

I lay back and began drifting off to sleep. The noise made be bolt upright. "Damn mosquito . . ." But as I opened my eyes, I saw that eight hours had passed. It was after 9 a.m., and the noise I had heard was that of all the birds who took breakfast at our pool.

Ira was still asleep. I quietly got out of bed and tiptoed over to the thing. I don't know what I expected to see. A pile of fried mosquitoes perhaps. I saw nothing.

"Now that was a good night's sleep." Ira was awake.

I looked at him. "Yes, and if you had listened to me, we would have used that *diffuseur* a long time ago."

Le Petit Voyage

THE ANCIENT SITE was set deep in the dark forests of the Maures mountains. It was a rectangular structure with expansive inner courtyards and high walls, more or less resembling the Alamo.

"What am I photographing?" Barbara asked, squinting through the viewfinder at one of the tiny, barren cubicles lining the exterior walls.

"I don't have a clue," I said.

Judging from the puzzled look of the occasional tourist passing by, I didn't think any of them knew either. But determined travelers were we, and like amoebas dropped into a Petri dish, we eventually coalesced into an informal tour group, drifting en masse into a moody courtyard with black crosses over unmarked graves.

"Muy interesante," remarked a woman from Spain.

"Si, tanti morti," observed a man from Italy, gesturing expansively.

The only nationality conspicuous by its absence was the French. This struck Barbara and me as odd since it was Monsieur Martignon who had all but demanded that we take a drive into the country and visit Chartreuse de la Verne, the attraction that topped his list of sightseeing suggestions. It had become his custom, after answering my questions about the care and feeding of La Chandelle, to end each telephone conversation with a touring suggestion. He seemed to have an endless repertoire of *"magnifique"* sights and *"fantastique"* restaurants we should experience in his Provençal countryside.

I had always thanked him, saying we would certainly consider his advice, but at the moment we were settled in and perfectly happy to relax at the villa. During our phone conversation this morning, however, his tone noticeably changed, and his sightseeing suggestion was accompanied by the word "must" instead of "should." Monsieur Martignon was clearly running out of patience. I had the feeling that if we returned to the United States without seeing Chartreuse de la Verne, he would write us off as jejune Americans and unworthy renters of his villa.

"She is a charterhouse from the twelfth century, surrounded by the chestnut woods—*elle est très belle,*" our landlord had said. He went on to explain that Chartreuse was a short drive from the historic hilltop village of Grimaud, where we *must* take lunch at one of his favorite French country restaurants. "*C'est un petit voyage,*" he added, presumably easing us into more serious junkets with this, a beginner's excursion.

"Okay," I relented. It was Sunday and we had nothing planned other than dinner in Ste-Maxime.

But there was irony in all of this: Monsieur Martignon had once admitted that when he and his family vacationed at La Chandelle, they all planted themselves at the pool or on the beach. He apparently believed that the fate of the French was relaxation, while Americans were destined to run around the countryside like madmen.

Still, a leisurely Sunday drive in the Peugeot sounded reasonable and we soon found ourselves cruising along the coastal highway. After fifteen minutes we turned away from the Mediterranean and toward Grimaud. The town nestled among vineyards and bucolic hillside farmland, with stunning views of St-Tropez and the coastline. Over lunch at Monsieur Martignon's restaurant-of-choice, I checked our guidebook for any references to Chartreuse de la Verne. Other than a dot on a circular route around the mountain range called, "Tour of the Massif des Maures," we found none.

"Grimaud is a branch on this tour," I said, holding up the page. "If we skip Chartreuse de la Verne and go the other way we can check out the village of La Garde-Freinet. It says here they have a pigeon museum with thousands of live, flying poopers on display, plus a video of the greatest moments in pigeon history."

"Flying rats," Barbara said.

"And then we can stop at the Village des Tortues. It's this sanctuary dedicated to saving a certain species of Hermann tortoise. Did you know that lawnmower accidents have driven them to near extinction?"

"No."

"It's tortoise mating season," I continued, "and I just might get the answer to a certain question I've always had."

My wife sighed. "Ira, we need to keep to Monsieur Martignon's itinerary. He's bound to quiz us later. Tell me what the guidebook says about Grimaud; it looks *really* old."

Barbara was right; it turned out that a valiant knight from the ubiquitous Grimaldi family of Genoa, the descendents of whom still rule Monaco, had been granted a fiefdom at this site as a reward for helping drive the Saracens out of the South of France.

So, after finishing lunch and paying *l'addition*, we climbed up to the highest point of the village and took pictures of an eleventh-century castle. Then we strolled along cobblestone streets lined with shops, enjoying the aromas of French pastries and coffee in the air. We could have easily spent the rest of the afternoon in Grimaud.

In retrospect, we should have.

Instead we drove westerly until we found the trail into the mountains. The Peugeot's chassis complained as we bumped and swayed along a meandering, rutted path that took us deep into the Forêt des Maures and to Chartreuse de le Verne.

Unlike many of the historical sites in France, this one had no guides. And without so much as a sign or a pamphlet, it's no wonder the building and the somber scene of the crosses in the courtyard baffled us. The image I had of a "charterhouse" was of a way station used in olden times to provide shelter to weary travelers, a roadhouse like the one in *Les Misèrables*, complete with a saucy mistress who entertained patrons with food, libation and song. But as I found out later, *"chartreuse"* or "charterhouse" means "Carthusian Monastery," a place where monks lived in cloistered solitude. This explained why the complex had been located deep in the mountain forest. But I never did learn why Monsieur Martignon had placed Chartreuse de la Verne so high on his "must see" list.

Since it was still the middle of the afternoon, we decided to take the short drive to Collobrières, a town known for making wine corks and chestnut products.

Collobrières didn't disappoint us. It had a picturesque humped-back stone bridge, *le vieux pont,* which straddled a river bisecting the village. Along the riverfront was a park-like setting where locals strolled or played *boules.* We bought some *marrons glacés—*

candied chestnuts—and ate and people-watched our way around the town.

I lost track of time until Barbara glanced at her watch. "We should start for home," she said.

Back at the Peugeot, I opened our guidebook and noted that Collobrières marked the halfway point on the "Tour of the Massif des Maures," so it was a tossup. "If we continue on the loop," I said, "we could make a quick stop at the turtle village."

"Let's go home."

"Okay, forget about the turtles. What about the pigeons?"

Barbara placed her hands on her hips and narrowed her eyes. "Look, let's just get back to the villa the fastest way; I want a nap before dinner."

I retrieved a Michelin map from the glove compartment and opened it on the Peugeot's hood. Locating Collobrières, I found what appeared to be a shortcut directly through the mountains.

My wife looked dubious. "Ira, that road is barely visible on the map. Are you sure it's paved?"

"Of course I'm sure it's paved. Just compare it with the dirt road to Chartreuse de la Verne. See? The map shows it dotted, while my shortcut is a solid line. Besides, I'll bet it's the road the Collobrièrians use to haul their corks and chestnut products to the coast."

Barbara was comparing the squiggly line on the map to the route in our guidebook. "Your 'shortcut' isn't even shown here," she said, waving the guidebook at me. "I don't have a good feeling about this. 'Maures' means 'dark and gloomy.'"

"Let's give it a shot," I said, folding the map. "If it isn't paved, we'll turn around. If the going gets rough, we'll turn around. I promise. Besides, it's Sunday afternoon and we'll probably have this remote road to ourselves." I emphasized the point because we had shared the highway to Collobrières with aggressive French drivers, and it had made Barbara nervous when they deliberately waited for blind curves before whizzing past us.

We fired up the Peugeot, found my shortcut, and plunged into the forest. The initial section of the road was paved and in fairly good condition. "See," I said, smiling, "this is probably one of those *bison futée*—crafty bison—routes the French use to avoid traffic." I was conveniently ignoring the fact that the road was barely wide enough to accommodate our miniscule rental car, and that unless the farmers hauled their corks on donkeys, I had been mistaken to think that this road would ever be used for serious trucking. I prayed we wouldn't be confronted with a speeding Frenchman coming from the opposite direction.

For some distance the road was relatively straight and I could safely motor along at 10-15 mph. Soon, however, it began to climb, and I had to slow to 5 mph to maneuver through the switchbacks. I was hoping the road would straighten soon, since at this rate, it would take an excruciatingly long time to reach the coast.

Our slow progress turned out to be the least of our worries.

Near the top of the mountain, the road was strewn with pebbles that compromised our traction. Simultaneously, the forest on Barbara's side disappeared and became a precipice that dropped two thousand feet to the valley floor. There were no guardrails, no roadside buffer, nothing to keep us from sliding off the mountain. Our right tires were literally inches away from the abyss. I reflexively braked, and the Peugeot came to a skidding halt. I heard the sound of pebbles flying off the road, and then silence as they dropped into nothingness.

For a long moment, only the idling of the motor grounded us to reality. Suddenly the engine sound was lost in a terrifying human shriek. "A-r-g-g-h!" Barbara shouted. "We're going too fast!" She had her eyes squeezed shut and her hands braced on the dashboard.

"We're stopped," I said, trying to remain calm. But my voice was breaking at the edges, my heart pounding inside my chest.

"That's still too fast!" Barbara yelled. Her neck muscles were bulging, her shoulders taut, her body stiff. My wife had clearly lost it.

I quickly glanced at the sheer drop immediately outside her window. Although there was the security of a mountain wall on my side, I was beginning to lose it myself.

"Turn around! Turn around now!" she ordered. Barbara was apparently hanging on to my earlier promise because there was clearly nothing else for her to hang on to.

"Okay, okay. Try and stay calm. I can't turn around here . . . nor do I dare back up. So we'll have to continue *slowly* until I find a place where the road widens. I'll get us out of this," I said without conviction.

Barbara turned to face me. Her eyes were as big as saucers and she was holding her right hand up to the side of her face to cut off the view of the precipice. "What if there's no place to turn around? What if the sun goes down and we're still on this donkey trail?"

She had a point about being stuck here overnight. There was no way I would move this car even an inch without the light of day. And with a rock wall immediately outside my door and an abyss just outside of Barbara's, we couldn't even get out of the tiny car to stretch our legs or go to the bathroom. If we became stranded on this mountaintop, we were in for a long, cold night.

"I'll drive slowly and *carefully*," I said. "And we'll look for a place to turn around. Even if we don't find one, this bad stretch of road should end soon, and then it will be clear sailing."

"Ha!" Barbara said.

"But I'll need you to help me: just focus on the road a few feet ahead of us. Watch your side and make sure the tires don't get any closer to the edge. I don't have the perspective you do."

"That's for damn sure!"

I put the Peugeot in first gear, and by riding the clutch and the brake, we motored along at a top speed of 1.5 mph. Suddenly, a horn honked loudly and I jumped. I reflexively hit the brakes and the engine stalled. In the rearview mirror, about a foot from our bumper was a Renault. The driver looked impatient as he motioned at us to pull over.

"Don't you dare!" Barbara sternly said to me, turning and glaring at the Frenchman.

"Don't worry," I replied, clinging to the steering wheel for dear life.

I started the engine and we inched along with the Renault on our bumper. The crazy Frenchman continued honking his horn, and periodically stuck his head out of his window and shouted obscenities. I was certain he was calling me a gutless, Sunday-driving American. I prayed he wouldn't contact our bumper and force us over the cliff. I had never been so scared, so tense, and so angry, all at the same time.

After what seemed like an eternity, the road widened a bit and the sheer cliff on my left became a sloping mound. I edged the Peugeot up the slope, hoping it would not slide sideways, or even worse, roll over.

Barbara was shouting, "Watch out! Watch out!" Her screams were intermingling with the Frenchman's wild honking, both of which echoed from the mountaintop, scattering birds and wildlife, and otherwise shattering the tranquility of the Maures. I stopped the Peugeot at a precarious angle and felt it shudder as the Renault passed us with perhaps an inch to spare. For good measure, the driver gave us the universal, one-fingered victory sign as he roared off.

Just as darkness fell, we found the coast and made our way home. I pulled up to the villa, switched off the engine, and the Peugeot and I both issued sighs of relief.

Barbara climbed out of the car and looked at me. "Do you want to know what a *petit voyage* is? It's the shortest distance from here to bed," she said, turning and disappearing into the villa.

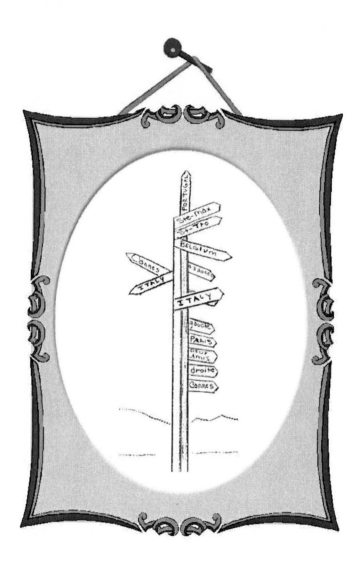

French Twists

A WAY FROM THE CITIES, the Provençal countryside is striking in its uniformity. Villas are beige stucco with red tile roofs and windows that have wooden shutters on the outside and curtains on the inside. Vineyards are neatly pruned. Beaches are well groomed. The land, like its inhabitants, seems polite to a fault.

On the other hand, once the French are traveling across their land faster than about three miles per hour, the rules of politeness are suspended and they are transformed into New York taxicab drivers. Actually, French motorists might be worse since New York taxicab drivers do not habitually force others off the road or drive on the sidewalk, scattering pedestrians in their wake.

I have formulated a theory about this behavior, a corollary to Newton's first law of physics that states: "A Frenchman in motion must remain in motion until he reaches his destination." This theory explains the dearth of traffic lights and stop signs in Provence.

Instead they have the traffic circle.

The traffic circle suits the French driving mentality perfectly because it allows motorists to drastically change directions without slowing down. Although *rond-point* is the proper French term for "traffic circle," I prefer the more descriptive phrase, *carrefour gyratoire*, meaning "spinning crossroads."

American visitors are fearful of traffic circles—and with good reason. The French expect drivers to join the *carrefour gyratoire* without the slightest hesitation, even when it's packed with traffic whizzing by at

111

100 kilometers per hour. And once in the frenzied flow, a vehicle must also exit without hesitation.

The penalties for *carrefour* crawling are severe. They include a cacophony of honking horns, shouted obscenities and rude hand gestures, all of which, if nothing else, are major distractions when a tourist is trying to choose the appropriate exit from among a confusing array of signs, all pointing in different directions, including up.

The saving grace is that a driver isn't required to ever leave the *carrefour.* For example, no one cared if I spun around and around until my morning's croissant was upchucked into a spiraling trajectory, or if I exited in the wrong direction and wound up in Portugal.

As a *carrefour* countermeasure, I included a portable Global Positioning System with all of my other electronics gear.

"Oh, no, not another gadget," Barbara groaned when I unpacked it at the villa.

"You're going to thank me for this."

"Sure I will," she said, her eyes rolling.

"Here's how it works: Before leaving the villa, I'll enter our destination into the GPS. You'll watch the screen and yell, 'Now!' when it's time to careen through our exit."

Barbara groaned again.

Actually, the system worked quite well and we rarely ended up in Portugal. Then, as time went on, we became accustomed to the tempo and signage of the *carrefour,* and now, after a couple of warm-up laps, we shot-put ourselves on course, and the GPS remains at home.

"Carrefour" also happens to be the name of a chain of mega-sized department stores called *hyper-*

marchés, a French invention that dates back to the nineteen sixties. These *hypermarchés,* which also include Auchan and Géant, are so ubiquitous that no matter which exit we take out of a traffic circle, sooner or later we wind up at one of these stores.

The French have mixed emotions about their *hypermarchés* because they are responsible for the demise of family-owned, neighborhood businesses. The personalized service and friendly conversation that make shopping more of a pleasure than a chore have been supplanted by discounts, enormous product selection, and robotic personnel. Unlike Americans, the French haven't yet become inured to the glazed-eyed clerk who disappears in the back to check the availability of an item, opts instead for a cigarette break, and never returns.

But visitors who rent villas are grateful for these *hypermarchés*, especially when one stop at the Carrefour in Nice or the Géant near St-Tropez is all that's necessary to set up housekeeping. This is particularly important when one must shop after staggering off the red-eye, because the rental lacks pillows, blankets, sheets and towels—in other words, any material that will come in direct contact with the renter's body.

Why villa owners provide just about everything else imaginable, except these necessities, remains a mystery. Are they afraid that foreign germs are so hearty that they will laugh in the face of powerful French detergents? Are they afraid of catching an incurable American disease, such as investing in Internet IPOs? From the patio of our villa, I periodically spot gray smoke spiraling upward from fires on the hillsides, and I imagine landlords—wearing gloves and dressed in protective body suits—burning the blankets and pillows their renters have left behind.

Fortunately for us, Monsieur Martignon is an experienced hotelier who is used to accommodating foreign guests, and apparently he has no qualms about stocking the villa with his hotel's towels and bedding—especially since it affords him a nice tax deduction. When we leave La Chandelle at the end of the season, Barbara piles the linens and towels in a wicker basket, and Monsieur Martignon takes them back to his hotel where they are laundered by the housekeeping staff and presumably labeled, "For use by Americans only."

Besides the lack of linens and traffic lights, there is another twist to life in the region that visitors must get used to: the rules regarding parking. Actually, in many places there are no rules, and parking is allowed in any space physically large enough to accommodate a car: on sidewalks; where the roadside widens ever so slightly; between bushes and trees; or wedged in a fourteenth-century cobblestone alley where the only practical way to exit the vehicle is to squeeze through the window and climb onto the roof.

But in other places, like the commercial districts of towns and villages, space is at a premium and parking indiscretions can be costly. To break its citizens of bad parking habits, municipalities have installed low-profile stanchions along the curb in front of the stores. These metallic mushrooms, which are painted in dark colors to blend into the background, are positioned less than a car length apart and will snare any motorist who attempts to park or drive on the sidewalk. When a wheel of a vehicle encounters the stanchion, it rides over its top and engages the car's frame so that no further motion is possible.

One day I was coming out of Le Tabac when I noticed a tiny Fiat, awkwardly canted to the left. A young lady rolled down her window and motioned me over.

"What seems to be the problem, mademoiselle?" I inquired.

"I don't know, Monsieur," she replied. "I have lost my traction."

She was correct, of course, as the Fiat's frame was firmly affixed atop a metal mushroom. "Just a minute," I said, somewhat superfluously, since the young woman wasn't going anywhere. I re-entered Le Tabac and asked Patou's brother, Daniel, to call a tow truck, the *gendarmerie*, or whomever it was one called in this circumstance. It must be a common problem, I thought, and there must be a prescribed solution.

I was right.

In fact, it seems the French have developed prescribed solutions to almost every conceivable problem. So rather than call for a tow truck, or a *gendarme* who would likely issue a ticket and otherwise throw his weight around, Daniel simply stepped out of the store and whistled to a group of five young men who were engaged in an animated conversation across the street.

The men sauntered over and walked around the car while nodding sympathetically to the mademoiselle-in-distress. Then Daniel and his friends positioned themselves strategically around the vehicle, and with a hearty, *"Un-deux-trois . . . HO!"* the young lady and her car were elevated and pushed back onto the road.

"*Merci,*" she said, smiling coquettishly.

"*De rien,*" the men replied in unison, waving as she motored off.

This brings us to the second corollary to Newton's first law: "A French driver at rest tends to remain at rest until disengaged from an anti-parking mushroom."

In St-Tropez they have motorized versions of these parking control devices that actually retract until they are flush to the ground. Tropéziens activate them with a remote control in their cars, allowing them to park in otherwise restricted areas. Needless to say, tourists are warned against standing astride retracted mushrooms while taking pictures of the kids.

Another parking twist is the French *payant* system. After locating a spot on a side street in Ste-Maxime, we got out of the car and noticed a sign indicating that we were in a paid parking area. This puzzled us because we didn't see any meters or anyone to receive a *paiement.*

Our confused look must have been a common sight in Ste-Maxime because in short order, a Frenchman in a Citroen stopped to assist us. I followed his finger as he pointed down the street to a machine about the size of a public mailbox. I thanked him, and Barbara and I walked over to investigate.

A sign above the machine read, "*Stationnement Payant Horodateur,* which in French techno-speak means, "Paid Parking Time Recorder." The sign went on to explain that payment was only required between April 1 and September 30, which coincides with the period when hoards of tourists descend upon the town. Oddly, it also spelled out, in great detail, all the *inapplicable* parking hours. For example, parking was free before 9:00 a.m. and after 7:00 p.m.; it was free between noon and 2:00 p.m.; and it was free all day Sunday. In other words, parking was free when the shops were closed, or it was time to eat.

For the actual *payant* period, you inserted one euro for each hour, and the machine issued a printed receipt for display on your dashboard.

"How simple and civilized," Barbara said.

"And Ste-Maxime isn't mucked up by ugly parking meters," I added.

This seemingly inconsequential parking lesson was a revelation. It was our first inkling that residing in the South of France was more like living in someone's house rather than in an actual country. If we needed information, it was comforting to know that our cohabitants—although complete strangers—were always willing to help. And in the rare instances when someone wasn't around, just knowing that the infrastructure was logical gave us the confidence to puzzle things out on our own.

But at the beginning of our first full season, we hadn't yet developed that confidence. Therefore, when we were confronted with a more complex parking issue, I failed to employ the appropriate logic and trouble ensued.

It happened at the end of our first magical night in St-Tropez, that delightful evening when we discovered El Mexicano, the Hôtel Sube, and the public *pissoir*. Hand-in-hand we strolled through the Parking du Port. And just as Monsieur Montignon had predicted, we easily located our lime-green Peugeot among a sea of silver-gray sedans.

In my back pocket, I found the ticket I had received when we had entered the lot, and like any other naïve American would do, I promptly drove to the exit station, about a quarter-mile away. Upon arrival, I noticed there was no attendant—only a freestanding rectangular box with a slot that said, *"Insérer Votre Ticket."* A gate arm prevented further motion.

"This can't be right," I said to Barbara. "There's no place to deposit money."

"Maybe parking is free," she conjectured, "and this ticket system simply prevents thieves from stealing cars. Go ahead and insert the ticket; see what happens."

I hesitated, worried that if the box swallowed the ticket, we might have a tough time proving we weren't stealing our own vehicle. There were few American tourists in St-Tropez, and *gendarmes*, lacking experience with us, might think we were just dumb enough to steal a garish, lime-green Peugeot.

Just then a big Mercedes sedan pulled up behind us, its headlights flooding into our car.

"Now you don't have any choice," Barbara said.

I prayed as I inserted the ticket and watched it disappear. After a several long moments, it was rejected summarily.

"There must be something we're missing," I said. "There must be a sign somewhere that tells us what to do. I'll ask this guy to back up and we'll retrace our steps." I exited the Peugeot and walked over to the Mercedes. It had German plates. "Could you please back up?" I asked the driver, a middle-aged gentleman. "I seem to be having difficulty with my ticket."

The gentleman immediately understood my problem. "You must pay first," he said in a stern, accented monotone. He pointed to a large kiosk, one of several sprinkled around the lot.

"Yes, of course, thank you," I said sheepishly.

The German released us, and we drove to the kiosk. In my headlights I saw a sign that read *"Caisse,"* which basically means "Cash Register."

"Now we're getting somewhere," I said, hopping out of the Peugeot.

"Really?" Barbara said. "To me it looks like we're still stuck in this parking lot."

Inside the dimly-lit kiosk there was a ticket machine officiated over by a homeless man. In one hand he held a cup full of change. *"Parlez français? Parla l'italiano? Sprechen sie deutsch? ¿Habla el español?* Speak English?" he inquired, all without pausing for a breath.

"Ah . . . English," I answered.

"Of course. Now insert the ticket to get the amount you must pay." He bent over and tapped on the machine's slot.

I did as he instructed. The ticket disappeared and the machine displayed "8 EUROS."

The homeless man nodded encouragingly as I dug into my pockets. But all I had in coins was seven euros.

The homeless man pointed to another slot for paper money. "It makes change," he said cheerfully, stepping closer, edging into my personal space.

I had several large notes on me, but in this isolated place I wasn't about to take out my wallet. Instead I moved back, opened my palm to the coins and punted: "It's all the change I have."

The homeless man nodded sympathetically. "No problem," he said, reaching into his cup and placing a one-euro coin into my open hand.

"No, I couldn't," I said.

"Please take it," he replied, flashing a toothless smile.

"Okay," I relented. "I'll catch you next time."

"Of course."

I inserted the eight euros, the machine made a printing sound, and the ticket ejected. I thanked the man and walked back to the car. Even in the dim light, I could tell Barbara was glaring at me. "Is it dawn yet?" she said, feigning a yawn. "What took you so long?"

"The ticket machine wanted eight euros, and all I had was seven, and there was this homeless fellow in there and—"

"—are you telling me you panhandled from a homeless person."

"I guess you could say that."

Barbara sighed. "This is getting worse by the second. Let's just *go*."

We drove back to the exit and I confidently inserted my ticket into the slot.

Again, it was rejected.

I put my hands on my head and sank low into the seat.

"With all of the delays, the amount is probably up to ten euros and climbing," I heard Barbara say. "Well, do something. Cars are lining up behind us. Again."

I sat up and reinserted the ticket. No luck. Either the amount was wrong as Barbara had surmised, or the ticket, which had gotten somewhat mangled by all of the handling, was no longer machine-readable.

At that point I noticed a button on the box and in desperation I pressed it. A muffled French voice crackled out of a small intercom. To me it sounded like: "*W-h-a-a . . . W-H-O-O-R . . . w-h-a-a-a.*"

I mumbled something back, which I'm certain was equally incomprehensible. Not knowing what would happen next, I turned off the Peugeot's engine and lights as a signal to the cars behind me that we weren't going anywhere, and they had better find another exit.

A few minutes later, a uniformed attendant walked over. His face was expressionless. Without either of us saying a word, he held out his hand and I gave him my ticket. With a key he opened up the box, placed the ticket inside, and pushed a button. The gate arm lifted, I cranked up the Peugeot, and we were on our way.

In subsequent trips to the Parking du Port, I have been careful not to stuff the ticket into my back pocket or otherwise manhandle it, and we had no further problems. And from the homeless Samaritan— whose kindness I repaid with considerable interest—I learned that after ticket validation, "the town gives you a twenty-minute grace period to," he laughed, "depart your *derrière* from the lot."

Even as we became seasoned veterans of French infrastructure, the memory of being trapped still lingers, and now, upon each successful exit from a French parking lot, people who may be peering into our car are puzzled by two adults who exchange high-fives when the ticket is inserted and the gate also rises.

Culinary Curiosities

WHEN WE BEGAN our quest for an "Enchanted April" vacation, learning a foreign culture was not on our radar screen. The culture didn't matter because the country didn't matter. If we had found a villa similar to La Chandelle on the Italian Riviera, or on the Estoril Coast in Portugal, or on the Costa del Sol in Spain, we would have considered our quest equally successful. But the reality is that setting up housekeeping and getting into the rhythm of villa life is impossible without some knowledge of the host country and its customs.

Shortly after settling in at La Chandelle we began to consider the world around us, and what we discovered was a land of cultural contrasts. Incredibly, the French have created a society where laissez-faire and conservative values co-exist; where children are venerated, while adultery is a way of life; where consuming alcohol is a daily ritual, but inebriation is frowned upon; where churchgoers dress stylishly for morning mass, then undress at the beach for an afternoon of semi-naked repose.

But these were things we learned in time. Initially, buying groceries and eating out were our primary preoccupations, so the cultural enigmas we first encountered were associated with food and wine.

"You need to sample this," I said to my wife after returning to the villa from one of my shopping forays.

Barbara closed her eyes for the tasting. "There's a hint of vanilla in here, with a touch of oak. Very low acidity," she remarked, running her tongue inside her mouth. "And there's an innuendo of spice, a note of

123

raspberries, and a velvety finish on the palette. Mmmm, I hope you have more of this."

"Of course. I'll get another white peach for you."

The *pêches blanches* and other fruit I brought back to the villa came from local farmers who have the strange custom of delivering produce when it's actually ready to eat. I was often forced to shop twice a day because the fruit, like the freshly-baked baguettes, had an expiration time measured in hours. In fact, we discovered that a warm baguette, purchased in the morning, showed signs of rigor mortis by dinner and, if left overnight, made an excellent baseball bat.

Farm fresh fruits and vegetables became a major part of our diet and led to the discovery of another food enigma: Although we seemed to be spending more time eating than doing anything else, we were always hungry. This posed a problem when we ate dinner out because of the French tradition of opening their restaurants relatively late.

"I'm dying of hunger here," Barbara said as we sat at a portside café in St-Tropez, sipping wine and killing time until the official dining hour. Suddenly I noticed a plate of something red and white move into my peripheral vision. I turned. At a nearby table, our waiter was delivering a fresh tomato salad with mozzarella and basil. "You serve salads?" I asked.

"*Oui, Monsieur.*"

"But there's no *carte* for food."

"Yes, that is true, but as you can see there is no *carte* for the drinks, either." The server grinned as if he were the sole recipient of an inside joke.

After he left I said to Barbara, "Do you think he's inferring that *any* dish is available, or is he simply saying the café's selection is limited to snacks and salads so they don't need a menu?'"

Barbara shook her head. "It wasn't clear. But we can certainly find out. Ask him for a steak."

I called our waiter over and announced in a deep voice, *"Nous aimerions deux entrecôtes, à point, s'il vous plaît."* I used my best French to make sure there would be no misunderstanding.

"Two steaks? Medium? *De cours, Monsieur.*"

The waiter disappeared and in seemingly no time at all, we were presented with two *entrecotes, pommes frites,* steak sauce, and a bottle of ketchup.

A few days later I decided to put the café's un-written menu to a *real* test. "This time I'm going to ask for sushi," I told Barbara.

She gave me a sideways glance. "No way."

"Watch me," I said as the waiter approached. *"Monsieur, ce soir, nous aimerions quelque sushi, s'il vous plaît."* I used my deep voice again, speaking casually and confidently, as if I were merely ordering a bottle of mineral water.

Our server's eyebrows lifted. *"Sushi?* Ah . . . what kind, *Monsieur?"*

I shrugged. *"C'est comme vous voulez."* Basically, I had told the waiter that it didn't matter and he could choose. But as soon as the words left my mouth, both Barbara and I knew I was asking for trouble. Waiters in Provence will often go to great lengths to please patrons, and I immediately regretted being so flippant about ordering raw fish at a sidewalk café.

"Are you crazy?" Barbara said. "What if he goes over to one of the fishing boats and we wind up with an eel wiggling on our plates?"

"Don't worry," I replied. "I doubt the fellow *really* knows what I'm talking about. After consulting with the chef, he'll save face by informing us they're out of sushi at the moment."

As the minutes ticked by, my confidence grew. "I've got him," I said to Barbara. "There won't be any sushi forthcoming."

Just then the waiter arrived. He was carrying a Japanese serving dish containing an assortment of fresh sushi and tuna sashimi, artistically arranged around *wasabi* and pickled ginger. He placed the dish in front of us and set napkins, chopsticks, and soy sauce on the table. He then cupped his hands and asked if we would like some *sake* to go with our meal.

We had not come to the South of France expecting to find *sushi* and *sake*. Like most visitors, we imagined painstakingly-prepared dishes with splendid sauces, aromatic herbs, and artistic presentations. We thought of superb wines, decadent desserts, and exquisite service. We thought of a people so serious about their cuisine, they would probably wage war with any nation that laid claim to their crown of culinary supremacy. So it came with some surprise when we discovered that most French dishes were standardized, as if dictated by government decree.

Prior to our first season, we had looked forward to experiencing the small family-run restaurants where the husband cooks while the wife acts as hostess and waitress. There are so many of these bistros along the Mediterranean, it was virtually impossible to travel more than a few miles without encountering a charming little place with pastel tablecloths, candles, and a view of the sea. Each one features *le menu,* which in France is not the menu at all but a multi-course, fixed price dinner. At around ten euros per person, including wine, service and tax, it was virtually impossible to dine at the villa for less money.

We ate bistro food quite a bit until one evening, as we sat in the Peugeot in St-Tropez' Parking du Port, I realized the novelty had worn off. We hadn't yet chosen a place to eat so I decided to call a special meeting of the Board of Directors of La Chandelle. "Where would you like to dine?" I asked Barbara.

"I don't know. You choose."

"How does Mexican sound?"

Barbara looked at me. "Again? You *do* remember where we are, don't you?"

"Of course. But the Provençal bistros always offer the same main courses: *loup, lapin, sole, daurade,* and *moules-frites*. It's as if the allowable *plats du jour* are licensed by the government."

"That's an exaggeration."

"And I can't experiment, either. Something from *la carte* that sounds tantalizing, like *rouget,* is really a plate of little red fish, complete with heads, tails, and whiskers. And because we're usually the first customers in the restaurant, the wife looms over us, watching like a hawk, so I can't dump the little fish bodies into her potted plant."

"Another exaggeration."

"Not by much. And if you order *coquilles St-Jacques* at one restaurant, it tastes pretty much the same at the restaurant next door, the one across the street, and every other Provençal restaurant from here to the Italian border."

"A gross generalization."

"Don't you think it's odd that in America, we choose a restaurant based on the distinctiveness of the menu, and then go to a fast food place if we want uniform fare? Here, we go to a restaurant if we want uniform fare and then choose McDonald's when we want a break."

Barbara sighed. "How about giving *me* a break?"

The special board meeting in the Peugeot went on in this manner until it was time to go to El Mexicano.

Actually, we did continue to patronize the bistros—but not quite so often. On one occasion, as a special treat, we tried a Michelin-rated restaurant. After being seated, we were presented with an *amuse-gueules*, a dish of savory morsels to "amuse the throat" while we awaited our first course. After the soup, the entrée was delivered with great fanfare. With a sweep of his arm, our waiter lifted a silver dome, leaving us eyeball-to-eyeball with a very large fish called *Gigot de Mer,* meaning "Mutton Leg of the Sea."

Dining is a serious business in France, so the use of whimsical food names surprised us. And once we were sensitized to quirky names on the menu, we began to see them elsewhere. On the road to St-Tropez stands an impressive amusement park. Colorful lights outline a large Ferris wheel, a roller coaster, and other rides, making the park look like a slice of Americana. I might have forgotten where I was except for the signs at the food kiosks. One pictured a large fluff of cotton candy identified as *Barbe-à-Papa,* or "Grandpa's Whiskers." Another showed a toasted ham and cheese sandwich called a *Croque Monsieur,* or "Mr. Crunch." Add an egg and it became a *Croque Madame.* A popular and sweet puff pastry is called *Vol au Vent* or "Flight to the Wind." I made a mental note to try one only *after* riding the roller coaster.

Descriptive food names can be brutally graphic. I learned this the hard way when I ordered bourbon at a sidewalk café. What I received was a pale amber liquid that was heavily diluted with water, and a bill for $12. Angrily, I told our waiter, *"Monsieur, ce bourbon est mauvais!"* With my poor command of the language, what I had actually said was that the bourbon was bad, like a naughty child. Subsequently, I learned that the proper phrase for a watered-down drink is *du pipi d'âne,* or literally, "donkey piss."

So what do the locals drink when they want something stronger than wine? To find out, we returned to the Café des Arts, a sidewalk café that caters to the neighborhood.

In short, the locals drink pastis.

Pastis is a serious drink if there ever was one, so it was surprising to discover how much playfulness is associated with the strong, licorice-flavored apéritif. "The Milk of Provence" is taken before lunch and after work. A shot glass is called a *momie*, literally meaning "mummy." The *momie* is often cut with chilled mineral water, turning the clear liquid milky-white. But if the *momie* is cut with grenadine, it becomes red and the patron has asked for a *Tomate*; if it's cut with almond and orange flower syrup, the patron is consuming a *Mauresque,* meaning "of the Maures mountains." The more adventurous will mix pastis and crème de menthe. This is called a *Perroquet,* or "Parrot," presumably because the mixture makes the drinker lose his train of thought and repeat himself endlessly. Finally, the combination of a *Mauresque* and a *Perroquet* creates both a lethal concoction and a torpid state known as *Feuille Morte,* or "Dead Leaf."

Some say pastis comes from *pasticcio,* the Italian word for trouble, as in troubled water. Others say it derives from the Latin *passe-sitis,* a thirst-quenching drink used in Marseilles as a remedy for the plague. But a little-known fact is that the liqueur makes an effective fish bait. One day a fisherman was having a lakeside *pique-nique* and accidentally knocked over his *momie,* spilling it onto a baguette. In frustration, he threw the bread into the lake, and suddenly the surface of the water foamed and frothed. When the baguette was gone, dozens of *goujon* lay floating on their backs with smiles on their faces. The fisherman took out his net, scooped up the anise-flavored *poisson,* and went home for a memorable meal.

Barbara and I tasted pastis and decided that the name really comes from the verb "to pass," which is exactly what we did. In fact, at first we stayed with *vin blanc* since we didn't want to risk the headaches we occasionally suffered at home with California reds. But as time went on we noticed that the French, even the elderly, freely drank *vin rouge* while dining out. Presumably, they weren't having adverse side affects, and that led us to wonder if we hadn't stumbled upon yet another food enigma.

"In the interest of science," I suggested to Barbara, "we should experiment. We need to know if there's something different about the constitution of the French, or if there's something different about their red wine. But let's ease into our study and start with one glass of red each."

Barbara agreed, but before long we were sharing a bottle at dinner without any problems. And whether it was rare Bordeaux or a *vin ordinaire,* it didn't seem to matter; we slept well and felt fine the next morning.

Some experts attribute the friendliness of French reds to differing levels of histamines, sulfites and tannins. Others ascribe it to generally lower alcohol content than their California counterparts.

Although there may be elements of truth to these explanations, we personally believed something else was at work. When drinking red wine, we adhered to the French tradition of drawing out dinner, drinking copious amounts of *l'eau minérale* with the meal, and taking a long walk before settling in for the evening.

We added rosé to our repertoire when we noticed that on hot days, the locals preferred pink wine to pastis. But unlike the American equivalent that tends to be sweet, Provençal rosé is dry and crisp. It's served with an ice cube, and the combination makes for a refreshing drink when the sun is strong and the air still. However, it's a serious *faux pas* to place an ice cube in any other type of wine, even white, because French proprietors pride themselves in serving their *vin* at the perfect temperature.

Clearly, we were quite naïve about the cuisine of France. We had no idea the people were playful in naming their dishes. We had no idea they had sidewalk cafés with a wide choice of menu items, but no menus. We had no idea that even when there were menus, the selection would be so uniform. We had no idea we couldn't ask for "French" fries, or "French" dressing, or "French" bread, because no one would know what we were talking about.

In other words, we had no idea that "French" food does not exist in France.

"French Not Spoken Here"

MIX IN ONE PART refurbished windmill, one part locally-grown ingredients, one part master chef, and one part multilingual staff, and you have the recipe for a Michelin-rated restaurant. One night, Barbara and I were sitting in the garden dining area of one such converted *moulin*, enjoying a leisurely and memorable meal. Around us, other guests chatted in melodious and incomprehensible French.

Over dinner, the question arose as to whether we should bolster our knowledge of *la langue sacrée* to feel less isolated—although we knew it would take a great deal of effort to understand and utter all of those lyrical, lip-puckering sounds the American mouth is ill-equipped to make.

But something happened that evening to give us pause.

It all started when I innocently informed the maître d' how we had thoroughly enjoyed our dining experience.

"Thank you," Claude replied in the precise and clipped manner of a Frenchman who had studied the Queen's English in the United Kingdom. "I speak on behalf of the entire staff when I say that any positive remarks we receive from our patrons are truly and deeply appreciated."

"Oh, I'll bet you get plenty of praise," I said. "There are few restaurants that can manage to combine a wonderful cuisine with such a fine ambiance and stellar service."

133

Claude nodded. "Yes, we get excellent feedback from the Americans, the British, the Japanese, the Italians, and the Germans."

"Wait a minute," Barbara said, gesturing at the guests in the dining room, "most of your patrons are French."

Claude glanced at the guests, leaned toward us, and lowered his voice. "If it were up to me, I'd put a big sign out in front that said, 'French Not Spoken Here.'"

He went on to explain that local patrons rip into his waiters every chance they get. He felt sorry for his staff because they were mostly college students working for tuition money. The twelve-hour days, coupled with a barrage of insults, made their lives miserable. Although they smiled bravely and were courteous as they delivered each dish, they often broke down and sobbed on Claude's shoulder in the privacy of the kitchen. "And those are the men on our staff," he added.

This took me aback. Without a single exception, the people with whom we interacted in the South of France had been extraordinarily polite. "I don't understand. Why are the local patrons so nasty?" I asked.

"In truth it is not just the locals. For the French people as a whole, nothing is ever quite good enough. It is part of our nature to demand perfection in all things. At the restaurant, we complain that the service is slow, the knife has a spot on it, the food tastes like *merde*, and the portions are too small. Even while you were enjoying your meal, these very comments were relayed to me by my staff."

"I had no idea," I said. "I had thoroughly enjoyed my plate of *merde.*"

"Me, too," Barbara said. "And since voices were never raised, I didn't know that people were complaining."

"Ah," Claude replied, waving his finger, "that is because it is a mortal sin for the Provençaux to raise their voices—particularly in public and especially at a fine dining establishment. The proper way for the French to complain is with a smile. And, as you can imagine, it is quite difficult to shout and smile at the same time."

Claude was right. I was mentally forming a picture as he spoke, and there was no way these two actions could occur simultaneously, at least not without drooling.

"So, when a patron is finished insulting the waiter," he continued, "a polite request is made for an appearance by the chef . . . ."

As Claude continued to talk, my mind played out the ensuing exchange:

Chef (approaching the table and smiling): "Good evening, Monsieur-Madame."

Mr. Patron (smiling): "Monsieur Chef, thank you for leaving *la cuisine* and visiting our table. How are you this evening?"

Chef (still smiling): "I am very fine, Monsieur. Your dinner was satisfactory I trust?"

Mrs. Patron (turning toward the chef and smiling): "I'm afraid not, Monsieur. The soup was swill, the salad wilted and tasteless, and the entrée was not fit even for the dog."

Chef (turning to the woman and still smiling): "Yes, of course, Madame."

Mr. Patron (continuing to smile): "Monsieur, I would like to grab you by your scruff and shove your face into the entrée so you can taste this *merde* for yourself."

Chef (continuing to smile): "Of course, Monsieur. And *I* would like to sever your wagging tongue with my meat cleaver, grind it into pâté, and shove it up your . . ."

Barbara squeezed my hand, signaling it was time to go. I thanked Claude for the cultural lesson, told him we looked forward to returning, and said good-night.

As we drove back to La Chandelle, I reflected on how our lack of fluency in French had contributed to a delightful and uninterrupted dining experience, and how it allowed our own conversation to be more vital and intimate.

But of particular interest to me were the maître d's remarks about the French demanding perfection in all things.

Suddenly it all made sense. Suddenly I knew why the countryside was so pristine, as if an army of covert cleaners descended *en masse* in the middle of night, tidying up, making certain the land was manicured, the roads were free of debris, the bathrooms were sparkling, and even the fruit was polished—all before the first light of day.

But I knew all of this came at a high price since perfection, by definition, is unattainable. Therefore, the implication of Claude's remarks was that the people who lived here could never be *truly* happy—

unless, of course, those people were a couple of Americans who were blissfully ignorant of the language.

The Face Plant

"GUESTS, LIKE FISH, smell after three days," Benjamin Franklin once said. But as an American, he presumably lacked the highly-evolved sense of smell of the French, a people who have assumed the heady responsibility for haute cuisine, fine wines, and perfumes. For this reason, I have always wondered if the French are more restrictive when it comes to the keeping of company and fish.

But unencumbered as Ira and I were by a finely-tuned sense of smell, we have had good success employing Dr. Franklin's three-day rule. The first day, the parties become adjusted to one another, with everything new and exciting. The second day is filled with activity, conversation and gaiety. The third day, loose ends are tied, hugs are exchanged and then, amongst teary goodbyes, you separate, always wanting more.

At La Chandelle, we decided to rigidly enforce the three-day rule because our concept of an "Enchanted April" vacation did not include operating a free resort with maid service, fresh cut flowers, gourmet meals, and tour guides thrown in for good measure.

Our only other rule was never to host more than one couple at a time in order to cut down our workload. So we had more than a little consternation when we suddenly found ourselves with extra fish in the barrel.

It started innocently enough. We had invited our friends, Karl and Karen, for three days of rest and relaxation at the beginning of their whirlwind European vacation. With La Chandelle as their first stop, they could recharge from their transatlantic flight, adjust to the time change, and be ready to tackle the rest of their trip.

But when a gray van skidded to a halt in our driveway, not two but three heads jerked forward in unison. We soon learned that the third head belonged to Rick, a friend of Karl's who had recently gone through a long and contentious divorce.

"My invitation was a spur-of-the moment, last minute kind of thing," Karl explained as he, Rick, and Ira hauled a massive amount of luggage up the driveway to the villa.

After we showed our guests to their rooms, Ira pulled me aside. "One extra visitor is no big deal. And any friend of Karl's is a friend of ours. Besides, the poor guy has been through a rough patch, and there isn't a better place for him to renew his perspective. It's no big deal."

I just looked at my husband.

Then while our guests unpacked, Ira and I set five places on the patio and brought out sandwiches and salads for lunch. But only Karl and Karen joined us at the table.

"Where's . . . ?" I began to ask just as I heard the van backing down the driveway.

"Rick is taking the van to *la gare* in St-Raphael to pick up Danielle," Karl explained. "She's arriving on the one o'clock train from Paris."

My mouth dropped, but it wasn't because I was aiming a sandwich at it.

"Who's Danielle?" Ira asked.

"Oh, she's this nice young lady Rick met after we

arrived in Paris last night," Karl said. "He invited her to join us, and she said yes. But it was too late to get her on our flight to Nice, so she took the SNCF this morning. She's French—but speaks English perfectly."

I was staring in disbelief at Karl.

"It was three o'clock in the morning," Karen interjected. "We were having nightcaps at the hotel bar when Danielle accepted Rick's invitation. Naturally, we didn't want to disturb you."

"How considerate," I said.

"You'll absolutely adore her," Karl assured us. "And by the way, our hotel in Monaco can't accommodate all of us until Thursday, so we'll be staying for a couple of extra days."

I heard a strange noise coming from Ira. He was choking on his sandwich and had to wash it down with water.

After lunch, we excused ourselves to do the dishes while Karl and Karen disappeared into their room to change into swimsuits. I took the opportunity to call an emergency meeting of the Board of Directors of La Chandelle. "So it's no big deal, eh? Now we're going to have to host four people—including two complete strangers—for FIVE whole days!"

"Shhhh, they'll hear you."

"I don't care. Did it occur to you that this Danielle person is probably a hooker? 'It's no big deal,' you say. And *I* say running a brothel for the better part of a week is the *best* we can hope for. For all we know, she's an axe murderess!"

"Calm down."

"I am calm—you should see angry! And while Rick is 'renewing his perspective' with Danielle, shall we serve them their meals in bed?" I was just warming up.

"Let's reserve judgment until we meet the young woman," Ira said, trying a different tact. "If she turns out to be an axe murderess, I'll 'axe' her to leave."

"That's not funny."

Just then we heard a vehicle pull into our driveway. By the time we walked outside, Karl was at the van and had the passenger door open, offering his hand to an attractive, long-legged young woman with straight, sandy-brown hair. He was smiling broadly. Rick was busy in the back of the van, retrieving her luggage.

"I am Danielle," she said as we approached. "But please call me Danni. I am happy to meet you." After firmly shaking hands she glanced around and said, "And thank you for having me—this is a lovely villa in a beautiful setting." The woman's English was laced with a lilting French accent.

"Don't mention it, Danni," Ira said. He was standing next to Karl and the pair of them had twin grins on their faces.

I held my husband back as the others moved toward the villa. "God, you are *so* transparent," I said.

"I was just being a good host."

"Yeah, right."

"Maybe this five-day thing is going to work out," Ira whispered.

"Yeah, right."

Later, at the pool, all of our guests, except Danni, succumbed to jetlag. While the young woman floated idly in our pool, her long limbs draped over the edge of a raft, Karen dozed and Rick slept behind the visor of his baseball cap. And Karl, with his golden hair and matching golden trunks, laid face down on another raft. I dragged a chaise lounge next to Karen and she opened her eyes. I remarked how rigid Karl looked, like rigor mortis had set in.

"We call that 'The Face Plant,'" Karen replied. "The only way he'll wake up now is if he turns over and falls into the water—but even that's not for certain."

Meanwhile, Ira sat on the edge of the pool and chatted with Danni. After twenty minutes, with Karen now sound asleep, I motioned him over.

"I was just being a good host," he said once again, as he settled into a chair next to me.

"Yeah, right."

"I found out some interesting stuff. Danni is the marketing manager for a telecom company. She's highly educated and hails from a wealthy French family."

"And somehow that's supposed to make me feel all warm and fuzzy?"

"Maybe not, but this should help: She adores Rick and our friends, but the only reason she agreed to accompany them was if she had her own bedroom. Rick is going to sleep on the banquette in the TV room."

"Great. Now we're going to have bodies sprawling all over the villa."

"You'll have to admit that having a guest speak fluent French might be an asset."

I just looked at Ira.

"If hosting this crowd becomes too burdensome, you and I can move into the Ermitage Hotel in St-

Tropez. We can get a nice room with breakfast for around $100 a night."

"Okay," I relented.

After a quiet afternoon by the pool, we gathered at the van at 6:00 p.m. for our planned Saturday night outing in St-Tropez. Karen and I both sighed as we watched Karl and Rick fall over themselves to help Danni into the backseat and sit next to her. The deal I made with my husband was that I would chauffeur us into town, and he would be the designated driver for the return trip.

Arriving at the Parking du Port, I hoped I conveyed the cachet of a seasoned *Tropézien* as I smoothly negotiated the ticket dispenser, casually tossed the receipt onto the dashboard, and expertly maneuvered into a tight parking space near the marina.

We headed to the exit, past wooden docks reserved for the smaller sailboats, and past an ornate nineteenth-century carousel not yet in operation for the evening. Our itinerary called for a round of drinks at the Café de Paris, a stroll through the town to the Place des Lices, another round at the Café des Artes, and then dinner.

"That was the tourist part of your trip," Ira said as we left the Place des Lices. "Now we're going to show you the *real* St-Tropez, the St-Tropez where the natives hang out." His announcement confused the Americans in our party who, having just been seated in a café filled with French-speaking people and a town square filled with *boules* players, believed that they *had* been experiencing the real St-Tropez.

"Actually," I explained, only 6,000 people reside in St-Tropez year-round. In the summer the population swells to 80,000, and many of the people you're seeing are Parisians who are considered foreign invaders by the Provençaux."

"Yes, that is true," Danni said.

We passed the beautiful Église de St-Tropez and I explained that in spite of church being a tourist attraction, most of the people who attended mass were also locals. "The music is the best thing," I said. "They sing hymns in French, and everybody sings, not just the choir." My enthusiasm was contagious, and as we followed Ira through the town's narrow streets, everyone said they were going to Sunday mass with me in the morning.

Suddenly, Ira stopped. "This is the *real* St-Tropez," he announced as he gestured at El Mexicano.

"You're kidding," Rick said, staring wide-eyed at the funky Mexican restaurant.

"No, I'm not," Ira replied. "There's actually logic behind this. St-Tropez' French restaurants make their money catering to tourists, and since repeat business isn't a major factor, they can let their standards drop. Although local residents generally avoid the tourist places, you'll find them here. For a Mexican restaurant to survive French scrutiny, it has to be extraordinary."

"Yes, I think that is true," Danni agreed.

We went inside and Karl ordered a round of Margaritas, with only Ira, our designated driver, declining. As we sipped and perused the menu, deciding amongst mariscos, enchiladas, flautas, and burritos, Karl noticed that one of El Mexicano's specialty drinks was a Long Island Ice Tea. "Since it's my fiftieth birthday, I think I'll have one," he said.

Karen leaned over and whispered to me, "He's been celebrating his fiftieth birthday *continuously* for five years."

A Long Island Ice Tea is an insidious and deadly concoction at any restaurant, but El Mexicano's version, in both size and potency, could have been used during the American Civil War as anesthesia for leg amputations. We all declined Karl's offer to help him consume it, but he seemed to manage this feat nicely on his own. Then, while we were finishing a delightful dinner, he called the waiter over and ordered another.

"You only celebrate your fiftieth birthday once in a lifetime," Karl announced, a twinkle in his eye.

"We're talking *serious* face plant," Karen quipped.

Karl downed his second Long Island Ice Tea in record time.

We asked for the check, which Karl insisted on paying, including a generous tip. El Mexicano's owner, in appreciation, brought out six complementary tequila shooters, each of which he slammed on the table to make them foam. Ira again passed, so Karl tossed down two. Strangely, other than speaking a little loudly and grinning from ear-to-ear, he was showing no ill effects.

At least, not yet.

After dinner, we were easy prey for Ira. "Let's climb La Citadelle," he said. "It'll clear our heads."

"Good idea," Karen said, looking at Karl.

"I'm game," Karl chimed in.

Now La Citadelle, a fortress dating back to the sixteenth century, is located atop the highest hill in St-Tropez, and is a delightful hike on a warm afternoon.

Paths wind their way around the hillside, transforming an otherwise steep ascent into a pleasant stroll. At its crest, the hill rewards visitors with a bird's eye view of St-Tropez and the blue waters of the *golfe,* all the way to Ste-Maxime. The Citadelle's strategic location and its battlements have protected St-Tropez from attack for four centuries, and it was now the site of a naval museum documenting France's long and prominent presence on the high seas.

But a leisurely stroll to the top of the Citadelle was not on Ira's agenda. Instead he decided on a frontal attack, a charge directly up the hill, apparently in honor of the Allied Forces who landed near here on August 14, 1944. The only problem was that our footing was impeded by high-heeled sandals and leather-soled dress shoes, the darkness that obscured the rocks over which we stumbled, and a strong wind whipping off the gulf against which we could barely stand.

With Rick assisting me, and with Karen and Danni keeping a close eye on Karl, we somehow scrabbled to a narrow plateau near the top. We were rewarded by a panoramic view of the lights of St-Tropez and the distant shoreline of Ste-Maxime. But even the anti-freeze coursing through our veins could not keep us warm against the chill of the evening wind, so we huddled together just long enough for Ira to snap a photo and document our group's crazy *attaque sur la Citadelle.*

Incredibly, Karl seemed fine as we climbed down the hill and hiked back to the parking lot. As we passed the carousel, its multicolored lights now illuminated, Karl stopped and said, "Let's go for a spin. It's my treat."

Karen was about to object when Karl handed the operator eighteen euros for the six of us and we climbed aboard. The carousel began to turn, its antique horses moving up and down to the buoyant notes of a calliope. Karl immediately stood on his horse and began waving wildly as if he were a stuntman at a rodeo. The operator left his station and began running along side, pointing at Karl and yelling something in French. Danni, on a nearby horse, shouted at the operator and he quieted down. She then dismounted and gently coaxed Karl back into his saddle.

Suddenly, our friend was not looking well. "How much did it cosht to get on thish caroushel?" he asked.

"Three euros each," Danni replied, returning to her horse.

Karl moaned, sank lower in his saddle and held his head in his hands. "And how much does it cosht to get off?"

As exciting as the idea of going to mass might have seemed on Saturday night, the reality of getting up early on Sunday morning was another story. I managed to coerce the group into the van with the promise of coffee and croissants at a sidewalk café before the service.

But by the time Karen got Karl out of bed, his limp body dressed and deposited into the van, there was no time left for breakfast when we finally arrived at the church. Karen and Rick, claiming severe hunger pangs, opted out, and then my husband, once again asserting his hosting duties, accompanied them to a portside café called Le Gorille.

That left Danni, Karl, and me standing at the entrance to the *église*. Actually, Karl was leaning against the building, so Danni and I, grabbing one arm each, guided him to a vacant pew where he promptly slumped forward just as the services began.

Forty-five minutes later, Karl stirred from sleep, poked me in the ribs, and asked if we could join the others for coffee. Looking into the red and tired eyes of the Patron Saint of the Face Plant, I could only agree.

We found the three heretic members of our party at Le Gorille. Bolstered by caffeine, they greeted us with mischievous grins and "See No Evil," "Hear No Evil," and "Speak No Evil" monkey poses.

Over breakfast Karl insisted that his vacation would not be complete unless we rented a boat and cruised the gulf. Last evening's wind had made the air and the water sparkle, and there wasn't a cloud in the sky. Rick confessed that he suffered from seasickness, particularly on smaller boats, and wondered if any of super yachts moored directly across from us might be available.

"Sure," I said. "Ira and I recently met a steward from England who worked on one of those ships, and he told us that most of the yachts aren't actually owned by the rich and famous. They're rented by the week. All we need is an extra $196,000."

"Whew," Rick exhaled.

"Look at it this way: you get nine staterooms with private baths; an outdoor Jacuzzi; a TV, DVD, stereo, fax, cell phones and Internet access; a sauna, gym, hair salon, and a baby grand piano. Did I mention that the price includes two 18-foot speedboats and a sailing dinghy?"

"Hey, I'll chip in," Karl announced, pulling out his wallet. But it was substantially thinner after his generosity last night, and he looked forlornly at the few bills remaining. "I guess I'll need to find an ATM first."

"I also should mention," I continued, "that the weekly rental just gets us *on* the boat. It excludes food, beverages, laundry, communications costs, fuel, oil, taxes, crew gratuity, water and electricity. From what we learned from the steward, for $196,000 we can just sit on the ship, and go nowhere and do nothing."

"What's Plan B?" Karen asked.

"The Thule 36," I replied. "She's a beautiful sailboat of the type and size I personally favor. Follow me."

I guided the group to the quai Suffren where the Thule 36 was moored. Standing before us was a classic sailing ship dwarfed by the super yachts on either side of it. But to me she was beautiful. Originally constructed in 1936 and now restored to her former glory, the Thule's mahogany decks were polished, its brass fittings glistened, and its wooden masts reached thirty feet into the air. It not only sailed the *golfe*, but did so with the elegance of a bygone era, and all for only ten euros a person, a great bargain.

We climbed aboard and joined several other tourists from various countries. After the ship motored out of the Vieux Port and into the gulf's open waters, Sylvana, the Thule's blonde and beautiful first mate, asked for male volunteers to hoist the mainsail.

Rick, who had taken Dramamine for his seasickness, was cured by being rendered unconscious and thus unaware that he was at sea. That left only Karl and Ira in our group to assert their manliness.

"C'mon," Karl said, pulling Ira to his feet. "Let's show the lady what we've got."

"That's what I'm afraid of," Karen remarked, taking out her video camera.

Karl and Ira, tugging arduously on the rope, began to slowly unfurl the sail. But after a couple of minutes of struggling, Karl let go of the line and dropped to the deck. This left Ira holding onto the rope for dear life, trying to preserve the scant progress they had made, barely managing to keep the fluttering mainsail from falling back into a canvas heap.

Meanwhile, the captain was roaring commands from the wheelhouse, yelling at Sylvana that the sail needed to be hoisted—*right now*—to avoid a collision with one of the $50,000,000 super yachts. The lithe first mate grabbed the rope from Ira and effortlessly raised the mainsail until it filled with wind.

"What happened?" I asked innocently as my husband plopped next to me.

"She used gloves."

"Yeah, right," I remarked as Danni giggled and Karen continued rolling her video. She was now capturing Karl, who had collapsed next to Rick. The two men had assumed matching face plants and would remain that way for the rest of the voyage.

Our two-hour cruise first took us toward Ste-Maxime and we were able to pinpoint the terracotta dot that marked our villa. We then sailed into the *Baie des Cannebiers* where Sylvana pointed out the region's natural wonders to her starstruck passengers in five different languages.

". . . to the left of Ms. Bardot's home," she was saying, "you see the house of Mr. Benetton and, beyond that, on the point, the home of Mr. Gucci. Nearby is the villa where the late Dodi Fayed and Princess Dianna stayed."

Although these famous landmarks were interesting, I suddenly realized that the *real* stars of the trip were the rippling waters catching the sun, creating a diamond path before us, and the gentle rocking of the Thule as water lapped against its hull. I felt a serenity that arises from gliding on the open sea, under broad white sails billowing against a blue sky.

As we returned to port, Ira and I chatted comfortably with Danni. She explained that she had met Prince Albert of Monaco at a charity ball and they had become friends. "When we leave your villa, we go to Monte Carlo where I will introduce Rick, Karl, and Karen to the Prince. If you would like, please join us. The Prince can guarantee us a ringside table at Jimmy'z, Monaco's exclusive disco for the jetsetters."

That evening, as we were lying in bed at La Chandelle, exhausted from the weekend's activities, I put my arm around Ira. "Isn't Danni interesting? What did I tell you? You have to keep an open mind about people visiting us. You're always so uptight about that silly three-day rule.'"

"Yeah, right," Ira said, mimicking me. It was the last thing I heard before we both executed the face plant for the night.

Jacques the Ripper

A SOUND . . . a distant buzzing sound . . . pulled me out of a deep sleep. I lay perfectly still, my ears exploring the villa. But only silence. Had I been dreaming?

A glance at the clock told me it was almost midnight. I climbed out of bed and entered the dining room, familiarity mastering darkness. I walked softly, not wanting to compromise my ability to hear.

A few rays of moonlight filtered through the sliding glass doors, just enough to silhouette the furniture. I peered outside, past the patio, beyond the band of blackness of the lawn, to the shimmering blue of the infinity pool. Everything was still. Nothing seemed out of the ordinary.

I was returning to the bedroom when I heard the sound again. A brief burst, a cross between a door buzzer and the ring of a French telephone. The pace of my breathing accelerated. I walked over to the phone and picked it up.

Only the dial tone.

I became fixated on the idea that someone was trying to get into our villa. There were many ways—a private entrance for each of the three bedrooms, the backdoor leading into the kitchen, and the large glass doors in front of which I now stood—exposed.

I could not tell the direction of the sound. I could not remember if we had locked all the doors. We had become secure in this quiet, virtually uninhabited neighborhood. Perhaps too secure. And now, ironically, that very seclusion was the threat.

I began turning on all the lights, my fear of being seen outweighed by a fear of not seeing. When I reached our master bedroom, I hit the wall switch and shouted, "Ira!"

My husband propped himself up on his elbows. "What is it?" he asked, squinting against the light.

"I heard a buzzing noise. Twice."

"The damn mosquito again? Get the spray," he muttered, collapsing back onto his pillow.

"That's not what I mean. Just listen."

Ira dragged himself up. After a moment the sound came again, this time steady, insistent. We both followed the buzzing to the television room. It seemed to be coming from a recessed panel in the wall. I opened the compartment and found a small handset inside.

Even before I had the chance to bring the receiver to my ear, I was treated to a barrage of incomprehensible French. When my attempts at *"Parlez vous anglais?"* failed, I turned to my husband. "There's an excited Frenchman on the line. I have no idea what he's saying. Here, you talk to him."

Ira took the receiver and after a few moments I heard him say, *"Attendez."* Then he hung up. "This isn't a telephone; it's an intercom. There's a man at the gate who wants to see us. Other than that, I have no idea what he's saying. But he seems desperate. I think we're going to have to investigate."

It was Sunday, almost midnight. I was not anxious to meet a stranger in these circumstances. On the other hand, it had become quite clear that this person was not going to have us alone.

We quickly changed our clothes, went out the door, and made our way down the driveway. As we reached the limit of the villa's exterior lights and plunged into shadow, I took Ira's arm.

The caller knew we were approaching. As we neared, he began again with his unrelenting, incomprehensible French. Although I could not understand his words, he sounded panicked.

He was not the only one.

We looked through our wrought iron gate. In the dim blue glow of the streetlights we saw a man in his twenties, his face, hands and pants dirty, his shirt torn. He was gesturing at the villa across the street, a home that had always been dark and shuttered, but was now illuminated.

For reasons that are not clear even with hindsight, we decided to unlock our gate and follow the stranger as he led us to the door of the neighboring villa. There we met Alain. He was tall and handsome, and even at that hour he was wearing dark slacks and a perfectly starched and ironed white shirt. His soft leather shoes were unscuffed. Only his tie had been loosened. When he realized we were American, he moved effortlessly from French to English.

He led us into his home where he explained that he had just come down from Belgium to check on a renovation project that was going on in his absence. He apologized for this Sunday night intrusion, but he had an important meeting in Brussels on Monday.

Then he turned to the young man. "And Jacques here is an apprentice carpenter who neglected to bring the chisel he needed to install a deadbolt in my new front door." Alain was clearly not pleased.

"So when I remembered seeing lights at Villa La Chandelle earlier this evening," he continued, "I thought, perhaps, that members of the Martignon family were visiting for the weekend. I sent Jacques to see if he could borrow the necessary tool. You understand that I cannot leave my house until it is secure, and I am not able to return here again before my vacation, at the beginning of July."

"Yes, I understand," Ira said, explaining that while he did not specifically recall seeing a chisel at our villa, he thought there might be something he could use among the tools kept in a storage area behind a bedroom closet.

I felt somewhat uncomfortable when Jacques followed us back to our villa, through the house to the guest closet, and watched as we pushed aside our coats to reveal a pocket door and storage area behind it. Jacques had no such discomfort. He opened the door, walked past paint cans and miscellaneous building materials, and began rummaging though a large red toolbox. Suddenly he turned and smiled, holding up the chisel he needed. He thanked us profusely. I stayed behind as he, Ira, and the chisel returned to Alain's villa.

Ira came back to find me in bed and under the covers. "I was scared," I told him. "Weren't you? I've been lying here thinking that we don't have a clue as to how to call the police or an ambulance. We don't know if they use 9-1-1 here. Jacques could have been Jacques the Ripper."

"That thought crossed my mind," Ira admitted. "As we followed the fellow into a strange villa, I had this queasy feeling in my stomach when I realized that very few people know where we are."

"We're such ingénues," I said. "We weren't even aware that there was an intercom at the front gate—"

"Okay," Ira said, climbing into bed. "Tomorrow we'll go to Ste-Maxime's tourist bureau and find out what we're supposed to do in case of emergencies."

"Good," I replied, turning out the light. I had thought about getting that information before, but my good intentions were always sublimated to the seduction of endless time.

The following morning, on the way into Ste-Maxime, we drove the Peugeot past Alain's villa, which was shuttered and quiescent as it awaited the owner's return in July. I calculated that, by now, the businessman was speeding through the northern part of France, bearing down on Brussels.

The building housing the tourist bureau was located in a park on the edge of Ste-Maxime's picturesque beach. The mid-June sun was strong, and even though it was still early, an amazing array of attractive women had laid claim to much of the sand. While I studied the brochures, posters, and schedules displayed in the front window of the bureau, Ira studied the scenery.

"I'll wait for you out here," he said absently, his quest for knowledge suddenly sublimated by the seduction of endless bronzed bodies.

That left me walking into the *Office du Tourisme* alone. The clerk responded to my question about security procedures by reaching under the counter and handing me the *Guide Pratique,* a fancy color pamphlet listing the emergency numbers—15 for the *Service d'Aide Médicale Urgente,* or paramedics; 17 for the *gendarmerie* or police; and 18 for the *pompiers* or fire fighters. Only the number 16 was missing, and I wondered what would happen if I dialed it. Since the brochure also contained listings for masseuses, pedicurists, hair salons, restaurants and wineries, I speculated that 16 was the emergency number for post-operative care, French style.

"That didn't take you very long," Ira remarked when I held the *guide* in front of his face to get his attention.

"If you need more time out here, I'm happy to go back inside," I said. "They have some great T-shirts and posters for sale, and I suddenly feel a case of the shopping munchies coming on."

"Never mind—did you get all your questions answered?"

"Everything but the name of a local doctor who speaks English. The clerk said that we could get that information at a drugstore. She also told me that French pharmacists are multilingual and that any of them should be able to help us."

We walked back into the commercial district and easily found a pharmacy. Inside, it was light, airy, immaculately clean and well-stocked. French cosmetics were tastefully displayed along with the toiletries and other hygiene products one would expect to see in an American drugstore. But unlike American stores, all drugs, even aspirin, were kept on shelves in the back. And, unlike America, French pharmacists could diagnose health problems and suggest appropriate treatment.

A tall, dignified woman in a white lab coat greeted us. As advertised, her English was excellent, and in short order I had the name, address and telephone number of a local English-speaking doctor.

Before leaving, I decided to pick up some decongestant pills, just in case my sinuses acted up on the flight back to the United States. I asked the pharmacist for a package of Advil Sinus.

The woman went into the back and returned with a strange-looking box and handed it to me. The labeling was in chemo-French, and the only word I could discern was the manufacturer—Boots.

Boots?

What kind of a name was that? Certainly not the name of a responsible pharmaceutical company to whom I could trust my pulsating sinuses.

I knew that American drug products were widely available in France so I tried once again, placing her box on the counter and pushing it back. This time I recited the words, "Advil Sinus," more slowly.

"This *is* what you want, Madame," the pharmacist insisted, pushing the Boots box back at me.

Suddenly I remembered that I had a single Advil Sinus pill remaining in my purse, still in its original package. I took it out and placed it next to her offering, pushing both products toward her.

The woman ignored my exemplar. "Still, Madame, they are the same."

"May I look inside?" I asked.

"Of course," she replied, opening her package and pulling out a flat foil of pills.

These are definitely not the same, I thought. My pills were tapered; hers were round and pudgy. Mine were shiny terracotta; hers were a pallid white. I shook my head. "I'm sorry, but they don't look the same to me."

The pharmacist tried to reason with me by citing her medicine's multisyllabic active ingredient. It sounded something like: *phenophalaxinahoxofoxyco-camine.*

I turned to my husband. "Ira, I will not swallow strange pills on a transoceanic flight. You had better do something."

My husband looked at the pharmacist, raised his palms and shrugged.

"I am *simply* being careful," I said sternly, crossing my arms over my chest and therefore returning his body language with some of my own.

Ira sighed and began comparing the label on my brand with the one on the French box. After a few moments, he pulled me aside. "Barbara, the ingredients and proportions are identical. *C'est la même chose,"* he said, trying to convince me in French since the pharmacist's attempts in perfect English had clearly failed.

At this point, I had no other reasonable choice but to uncross my arms, thank the woman for her patience, and buy the pallid pills.

After leaving the store, we quickly located the office of the English-speaking doctor in a quiet tree-lined neighborhood. All of our missions were accomplished and we would be home in time for lunch. But a few minutes later, as we pulled up to La Chandelle, surprise replaced our self-satisfaction. Across the street, the gates of Alain's house were wide open, and his front door was ajar. Did the Belgium businessman return because he had second thoughts about his villa's security? Did young Jacques bungle the lock installation only to have the home summarily robbed in broad daylight?

Ira climbed out of the Peugeot and took a few steps onto Alain's property. He called out, "*Allo!*

Allo! Èst-ce qu'il y a quelqu'un? Is anyone home?" He listened for a few moments and then returned to the car.

"There's nobody around—or at least, no one is responding."

I removed the *Guide Pratique* from my purse. "Let's call the *gendarmes.*"

Ira glanced at his watch and thought for a moment. "Maybe we should wait a while. It's possible that workers arrived while we were away and they're taking a lunch break. Didn't Alain say something about having his home renovated?" My husband then pointed at a large cone-shaped mound of sand, just to the left of the villa's gate. "It wasn't there this morning."

"All right," I said. "We'll check again in an hour. If the house remains empty, we dial 17."

"Okay."

As we were finishing lunch, we heard a vehicle pull up across the street. Ira and I hurried to our gate and watched. This was not a clandestine operation what with all manner of equipment and workmen moving in and out, the words "Piscine Automatique" boldly emblazoned on their overalls and truck. After a few moments, one of the men approached the mound with a wheelbarrow and shovel.

And then the next day, and everyday thereafter, the truck returned and the pile of sand shrank in size—for Alain a swimming pool to be completed before his return in July—for us an inverted hour glass measuring what remained of our month in the South of France.

Argent Noir

"**B**LACK MONEY. Is that like the Black Market?" I whispered to the back of Ira's head. I was in the rear seat of a sport utility vehicle that was attacking the steep hills of Ramatuelle, lunging in and out of potholes, dirt and rocks flying. Either ignoring me, or unable to hear above the din of pummeled steel, Ira didn't answer. Instead, he continued his conversation with the good-looking, English-speaking real estate agent who was our chauffeur. Philippe was using one hand to steer and the other to punctuate his dissertation on Trope-ziénne real estate with exaggerated gestures. I was certain that if I were ever to see La Chandelle's pool again, it would have to be in my next life. Higher and higher we climbed until finally skidding to a stop in front of a three-story villa perched atop a mountain. The wind whistled loudly past the windows of the SUV.

"This is a five-bedroom home," Philippe said as we piled out. "Notice there is a 270-degree view of the sea and the remaining 90-degrees is of protected parkland. There are no other houses nearby."

I can see why, I thought as the wind howled and I flattened myself against the SUV. *There is no way I would live up here.*

"This is gorgeous," I heard Ira remark as he stood on the wind-sheltered side of the vehicle.

I slowly made my way around the SUV, then quickly stepped over to my husband and put my arm firmly around his shoulder. Mistaking this as an act of affection instead of traction, he squeezed my hand

and we followed Philippe into the house, through a tastefully decorated living room, and then through a set of French doors that opened onto a patio.

As we continued our tour, I felt as though we were on top of Mont Ventoux, the mythical source of the mistral.

How had we arrived here? I wondered.

The answer was curiosity. Although we loved La Chandelle and its surroundings, we had had time to reflect and we were now wondering how our villa, and the amount we were paying, compared with other rentals. The neighboring properties, although all Provençal in architecture, were distinct in design and layout. Roughly similar in size to La Chandelle, the average lot measured about a half acre and the average house about 2000 square feet. Mature trees and shrubbery gave each villa a measure of privacy—not that it mattered much since the high season had not yet begun and all the villas were shuttered. The properties were well groomed, and reminded us of Bel Air or one of the other upscale neighborhoods nestled in the hills overlooking Los Angeles.

The homes on the ridgeline above La Chandelle enjoyed spectacular, unobstructed views of the Mediterranean and, from that vantage point as far as the eye could see, villas speckled the hills that gently rolled along this part of the coast. We had learned from Monsieur Martignon that although some of these properties were locally owned, most belonged to businessmen, diplomats, and government officials from Paris, Milan, Brussels, and the other large cities in Europe. Owning a second home by the sea, Monsieur Martignon explained, was a measure of a family's stature and success.

A week ago, at lunchtime, we had driven down the hill and shared a pizza at a seafront restaurant. "In retrospect," I had told Ira, "La Chandelle is a perfect set-up for us. It offers the solitude of the countryside I was looking for, while St-Tropez and the other coastal towns offer the diversions you were after."

"Hmmm," he said, deep in thought.

"What is it?"

"I agree with you about this area—it *is* perfect. But how do we know our particular villa is 'perfect'? Frankly, I was taken aback when Monsieur Martignon told me how he wanted to get paid."

"Not me," I said. "I thought he was funny— 'American dollars in the sock. When you go, leave the money in the refrigerator. Cold cash.' Then he had laughed heartedly at his ability to joke in English."

"Maybe that's the custom, but how do we know?" Ira asked. "We could be participating in a tax avoidance scheme. I'm thinking we should find a legitimate real estate agent, check out a couple of other properties, and learn what rentals really cost."

The pool at La Chandelle was a giant magnet for me, and the last thing I wanted to do was traipse over the countryside looking at rentals.

We drove back up the hill and Ira went villa hunting over the Internet. There was no end to the number of sites he was able to locate offering "Luxury Villas on the Cote d'Azur." But there was no way we were going to assess a place sight unseen. So we jotted down some notes and used our cyberspace information as a point of reference.

I settled into a lounge chair by the pool and began reading English language magazines that we had picked up after lunch. I thought that I had struck gold when I found one entitled *French Riviera—Dream Homes to Rent* . . . that is, until I began examining the fine print. The caption under one pictured estate read, "10 bedrooms, 10 bathrooms, with 6 bedrooms for house staff. 2 elevators. Covered garage for 5 cars. Heated indoor and outdoor swimming pools with hammam and pool-house. Available in July and August for $25,000 per week."

Other homes were more modest in size, and were offered without house staff and a hammam: "The villa comprises 7 bedrooms, 5 bathrooms and a large, free-form swimming pool. Ideal for a relaxing vacation on the Côte d'Azur. Sheltered from noise and prying eyes. Only $40,000 per month."

As I paged through the magazine I noted that all of the homes were much larger than La Chandelle and the surrounding villas, and had much more space than we needed for just the two of us and the few friends who dropped by. And most were near the larger cities of Nice and Cannes, while we were quite happy to be near the smaller resort towns.

So we made a list of what we were looking for, those aspects of a villa that had grown indispensable: two bedrooms, two baths; swimming pool; sea view; and a well-equipped kitchen.

We did not have a clue where to find a knowledgeable *agent immobilier*, so the next morning, under another clear blue sky and warm and balmy day, we set out for St-Tropez' main *Bureau de Tourisme*. We found it on the road to town, adjacent to a lot full of life-sized replicas of prehistoric dinosaurs. Beyond the dinosaurs was the amusement park and, beyond that, immaculately groomed polo grounds with players in elegant outfits, riding magnificent sable-colored horses. A sign identified the area as *La Foux*, or "The Crazy Ones," and the mixed uses seemed Fellini-esque, as if Gallic sensibility—and the rules that governed the well-ordered planning we had seen everywhere else—had been suspended. I did not find this setting to be very encouraging.

We entered the office, approached the counter, and were greeted by a young woman who spoke English among other languages.

"Yes, we have many books of places you can rent," she said. "If you would like, you can make the arrangements directly through this office."

Wow, this is way too easy, I thought.

The woman stacked three huge black binders on the counter, pushed them towards us, told us to pick whichever villa we liked, and excused herself to take a phone call.

I grunted as I lifted the first album and plopped into a seat in the reception area. Ira joined me and leaned closer as I began thumbing through pages and pages of color photos and descriptions. We had been right; there were literally hundreds of listings in the vicinity of Ste-Maxime, and hundreds more in the nearby towns—all priced comparably to our villa. The sheer quantity was overwhelming, and it would have taken us the rest of the day just to get through the first binder.

I turned toward Ira. "Angst," I said.

My husband stood when the woman set the phone down and returned to the counter. "Excuse me. Can you recommend a real estate agent?"

"It is not permitted to recommend *agents immobiliers*, but I can photocopy for you a list."

The list itself was pages and pages long, and it was impossible for us to choose one real estate office over another, or one area over another. We were getting nowhere fast, and I felt as if we were riding on the carousel in the amusement park next door.

"Can you tell us which offices represent properties specifically near St-Tropez?" Ira asked.

"Yes, I will mark for you the ones."

The list was still long. But we chose an agency located on a road we knew that ran through beautiful, manicured vineyards. It had always amazed us that expansive farmlands could exist in such close proximity to the urbane chic of St-Tropez.

We located the office and entered. Ira approached the realtor and hesitantly asked, *"Parlez vous anglais?"* Even though we were only a few kilometers from an international crossroad where people switched between English and French as easily as super yachts slipped in and out of port, we were in the country now and, from past experience, I knew Ira did not expect an affirmative response.

The large, middle-aged man to whom his question was directed stared down at us, his gaze neutral, his face impassive. "Sure," he said easily. "What can I help you with?" As soon as he was able to glean that we were interested in villa *rentals*, as opposed to villa *purchases*, he quickly directed us to the small office of his son Philippe who, he told us, "handles these matters."

The young man offering his hand appeared to be in his early thirties. As with Le Tabac, I noted that we were once again dealing with a family-owned business.

Efficiently, Philippe interviewed us, learning that we were looking for a two-bedroom villa with a pool and a view of the sea, nearer to St-Tropez than our current villa. "I am afraid there is no such thing. If you wish to have a pool, you must take three or more bedrooms. With the cost of land near St-Tropez, it is not economic to have a pool with a smaller villa."

He explained that although he was mainly involved with the sale of homes, he handled rentals for some of his clients. There might be a few that we would be interested in, but he would need about a week to contact the owners and make arrangements for our visits. He scheduled an appointment with us at 11:00 a.m., in seven days' time, and we were on our way.

And so, one week later, while the winds of Mont Ventoux howled, I was seriously doubting that any questions we had about villas would be answered here, when the front door, which we had left open, thunderously slammed shut, shaking the entire house.

"All the doors are steel reinforced," Philippe said cheerfully.

"That's nice," I said. *There is no way I would live up here.*

Below the patio the land was terraced, ending at a large pool surrounded by a perfectly trimmed lawn. Beyond the lawn was a steep drop into the diamond-studded Mediterranean Sea.

"This is almost spiritual," Ira said, above the wind.

Because the wind could fling you off the cliff to your death, I thought. "Let's see the rest of the house," I said.

We followed the agent upstairs. The guest bedrooms were surprisingly small for a villa this size, with just enough space for two single beds and a dresser. A slightly larger master bedroom opened onto a balcony with the same expansive view we had seen from below. In the basement, there were storage closets, a wine cellar, and a utility room with a washing machine. There was no clothes dryer, but neither was there one at La Chandelle, so I presumed the French were content to place their faith and wet clothes in the sunny weather of the Côte d'Azur. But as the gusts continued to slam shut every door we opened, I knew that drying our clothes would not be a problem up here. In fact, I fully expected that our clothes would dry quickly as the wind ripped them from the clothesline, and they flew in the jet stream alongside the daily Air France flight from Nice to Paris.

Back on the main floor we toured the kitchen, which was well stocked with fine china, a variety of cookware and kitchen utensils, and a dishwasher, stove and microwave oven. "This kitchen would certainly make it nice to stay here," Ira said.

Right. In my next life as a mountain goat.

As we headed out the front door and leaned into the gale, I now wondered if there was so much wind on such a perfectly beautiful day, what would this place be like during one of the area's infamous mistrals?

The agent used our walk to his SUV as the opportunity to discuss the value of real estate in the South of France. "In Haute Provence, in the Luberons, you can find a nice house for $250,000 American dollars. But here, on the coast, it will cost five, maybe six, times that amount. "Where you live, how much would this house be?" he asked Ira, barely able to hide his pride in representing what he believed to be some of the most expensive real estate in the world.

"On the California coast, many times this one," Ira answered.

Philippe said nothing, but I sensed some deflation as we returned to his upscale SUV.

Our next stop, a three-bedroom house, was half-way down the mountain. Here, the wind was more like a strong breeze, and the sea view, although not as awe inspiring, was still marvelous. Situated on two levels, the villa had the advantage of having a separate wing for guests. Like the prior rental, the bedrooms were small but functional, and the décor and amenities—sans clothes dryer, of course—seemed more than adequate.

As we drove back to the agency, Philippe told us that the first villa was renting at $12,000 for the month of June, and the second went for $7,000. Doing some quick calculations, I figured out that the monthly rents were about 1% of the property's value. Philippe explained that the prices included all utilities and a groundskeeper who came several times a week to maintain the pool and landscaping. Telephone charges would be extra. He told us that these rates were higher than in Ste-Maxime because of the properties' proximity to St-Tropez and its beaches.

"If we pay in cash, how much of a discount do we get?" Ira asked as he leaped off his high moral ground without a parachute.

"None. Everybody must pay in cash," Philippe replied matter-of-factly.

He explained that, for a one-month rental, a 35% non-refundable deposit was required, with the remainder due upon arrival. "We take a check for the deposit, but we do not put it in the bank. When you arrive, it is returned, and you pay the entire amount in cash."

"But we can only bring $10,000 into the country. How do you get around that?" Ira questioned.

"A cash advance on your credit cards when you get here to make up the difference, and we tear up your check," Philippe explained. "The tax rate here is about 75%, so we have this black money, *argent noir,* or we could not afford to live.

"The same with my salary," the agent continued. "My father pays me what is about $30,000 in the United States, and the rest I receive in cash and do not pay taxes on. And the same when you sell a house. We advertise it at one price. The seller grumbles and pays taxes on the advertised amount, but he gets the rest under the table with, *voilà,* no taxes."

I asked Philippe if the rental included pillows, blankets, sheets and towels.

"No. You can rent those things, but I do not recommend it. It is too expensive. So most of my clients buy what they need when they get here, and I store it for them when they leave."

As we rolled off the mountain and skidded to a stop at the agency, Ira thanked Philippe for his time. Walking to our car, he said, "That sure was an education in French economics. *Argent noir,* black money, cash."

"I thought it was an education too. I learned that there is no way I would live in a place, even nearer to St-Tropez, and even with a 270-degree *vue de la mer,* if I have to scale a mountain when I go to the grocery store in the morning or drive home from dinner at night, and tether myself to the patio to keep from getting blown off the mountain during the day."

"Life's a trade off," Ira said. "You have to consider what's important to you."

"Right. I've thought about it. Let's go back to *our* villa. With its sheets and its towels and pillows and blankets." And built on a hillside that I could scale in a lime green Peugeot. Cash in the sock didn't sound like such a bad deal after all.

Le Club 55

THIRTY EUROS EACH? To rent a mat and umbrella. Not even a towel. This may not be such a good idea," I said.

But Ira reasoned it was a beautiful day, eleven o'clock on a Sunday morning, and Club 55 was supposed to be a legend and the toniest beach club around. "Sixty dollars is not going to break us, and we can keep the stuff all day. We're here now, so let's go in."

I was the one who had first read about *Club* (pronounced "*cloob*," lips in smooching formation) *Cinquant Cinq*, its genesis the film *And God Created Woman* starring Bridget Bardot, filmed in St-Tropez in 1955. The movie crew had hired the wife of a local ethnologist to cater its lunches on the beach, her *cantine* food was great, and Club 55 was born.

As Ira and I walked around the bamboo fence that separated the parking lot, any cost concern was quickly displaced by decorum distress. We had seen such clubs on all the beaches, but had never visited one. My worries increased when a gorgeous young man approached, asking questions in what was, for me, unintelligible French. As I quickly glanced around, I noticed that dozens of casually sophisticated individuals had already staked their claim to patches of towel-protected sand.

"He wants to know where you would like him to place our mats and umbrella," Ira said.

Switching to English, the young man looked at me. "You can choose."

I was certain that my glazed-over eyes and non-responsiveness were now revealing the discomfort I was trying so desperately to conceal. Here I was at my first French beach club. We had chosen the trendiest one. It was up me to select seating location because I am so opinionated on the subject. Meanwhile, the hunk is smiling and waiting, and I do not know what to do. Should we sit near the water, or in back where swimmers would not disturb us? Should we position ourselves near the wind-protected bamboo fence to our right, or invite the breezes to our left? Are all the cool French people staring at me, or am I just imagining one hundred piercing eyes? And I had so wanted to appear sophisticated.

I pointed to the water and away from the fence with all of the aplomb I could muster. The hunk, carrying both mats and umbrella, moved forward briskly. Now standing in front of everyone, he asked how we wanted our mats positioned on their awaiting wooden frames and how we would like our umbrella tilted. At this point, I abandoned logic and replaced it with the expediency of feigned experience. "This way and that way," I answered.

Ira paid the young man who smiled, very white teeth against very tanned skin, then turned and disappeared into a sea of blue and white striped umbrellas.

I fell to my mat, not caring at this point whether I was facing toward or away from the sun—toward or away from the sea—just so I could give the appearance that everything was exactly as I had planned.

Now came the next test. With sunglasses on, I studied what my guidebook had described as the "coast's showcase for fun, sun, fashion and glamour." What do my neighboring sunbathers look like? What are they wearing, here in the same beach area, as Tropeziénne legend goes, that a woman was first seen in a string bikini? Are the women topless? What are they doing? I had already suffered angst preparing my Club 55 wardrobe. Had I passed? I certainly had plenty of beach experience, which included France. But this was different.

The first thing I noticed was that no one was looking at us. I didn't know if that was good or bad. The second thing I noted was that while there were some couples scattered about, most were families, usually three generations, with a few nannies thrown in for good measure. I reasoned that this was the Sunday family outing, Tropeziénne style. As naked children played, always under the watchful eye of a relative or *au pair*, family members chatted quietly. Most of the mothers and grandmothers were topless, many rolling their one-piece suits to their waists while sunbathing, only covering their breasts when walking about. My lack of gold jewelry and make-up distinguished me from about half of the women—

"Pretty nice, huh?" Ira interrupted.

I could not believe my husband. How could he be so relaxed in the face of the issues to be solved, investigation still to be done? I sat facing him as he reclined back, an opened book by his side, not a care in the world, looking out over the *Baie de Pampelonne*. So I turned and my eyes caught exactly what Ira, in a clear understatement, thought was "pretty nice." Anchored approximately three hundred yards from the beach was a sampling of the super yachts we had before only seen docked across from the Café de Paris in St-Tropez. Putting aside my incomplete sleuthing, time passed as Ira and I discussed the pros and cons of each yacht design, deciding which of these $200,000-a-week-boats *we* would choose—I selecting those that most resembled the brass-adorned wooden yachts of the 1930s, and Ira favoring the sleek, high-tech vessels sporting helicopters and antennae suggesting a plethora of electronic gadgetry.

When small motorboats began ferrying the occupants of the super yachts to the small wooden dock nearby, we were confused. Was it a tour group? "One hour and only ten euros, and you too could experience the life of the rich and famous."

We watched those disembarking stroll toward Club 55's restaurant. At the same time, the people around us began to stand and prepare for lunch. I looked at my watch: it was 1:00 p.m. I had learned to monitor the comings and goings of the French, and at the cafés, restaurants and discotheques, patrons tended to arrive and depart at standardized times.

Tradition was alive and well on the Côte d'Azur, and what we had just witnessed were the motorboats Club 55 had dispatched to transport the super yacht passengers to lunch. Through pure luck, we had made 1:30 p.m. reservations when we first arrived, avoiding the fate of other guests who were turned away.

But I had my own problems. I never anticipated that eating was going to be such a big deal during our day at the beach. What was the appropriate attire for this event? It was becoming increasingly hard to remember that I had been quite cavalier about my wardrobe when I was at home. But here I was motivated not simply by insecurity but by knowledge that there were unwritten rules, reinforced by the uniformity of the apparel moving past us. For men, the clothing of choice consisted of loose-fitting linen pants, cotton shirt, sandals and Panama hat. The women coordinated with linen skirts or dresses, which skimmed the body (the swimming suit having been modestly and adroitly removed on the beach) to mid-calf, and sandals and roll-brim straw hats. The colors covered the range from cream to beige. As the maître d' seated us amongst these tables of family and super yacht guests, Ira and I found ourselves suitably, although not so uniformly attired, vowing that before our next visit we would definitely master the dictates of beach fashion.

Maybe it was the wine. Or maybe it was the soothing, low murmur of the voices at surrounding tables. But I think it was the olive grove. The olive grove that formed our dining room, its muted greens and browns blending with its floor of sand, creating both a pervious partition from the sea and dappled shade from the sun. The olive grove from which a long and leisurely lunch segued seamlessly and time-lessly into our return to the beach.

Walking to the water's edge, I noticed for the first time that day just how beautiful and clear the water was, hues of turquoise blending to the horizon. Looking to our left and to our right, neighboring beach clubs were recognizable by the colors of their umbrellas, distance blurring details, creating a rain-bow's continuum along the *Plage de Pampelonne*. Re-turning to our beach mats, my mind unconsciously occupied by the water, the boats, the absent-minded flipping of pages of one of the magazines I had brought to fill the hours, I had entered the languid rhythm of *la plage*.

I Painted a Pot of Flowers

I IMAGINE. I always have.

As we drove to Villefranche, I asked Ira what he imagined it would look like. "I don't know. I'll see when I get there."

Not everybody imagines. Not in the same way at least. But for me, words evoke images. Images can become realities. And reality can create a new image.

On that particular day, as we made our way along the coast, the air was warm, my mind wandered, and I reflected on why it was that out of the events forming our lives, some stood out, while most were forgotten.

I remembered having the flu when I was a child. I was rarely sick, but this time a persistent fever had kept me in bed for two weeks. After I had read every book, magazine and comic in the house, I started to do pencil sketches of my novels' illustrations and of comic book characters.

I remembered my mother complimenting me on my drawings, and the unusual thing was that the compliment stood out more clearly than most others I had received. Then time passed, I grew, my perspective changed, and my art was put aside.

Until St-Tropez.

Over the centuries a willing courtesan to those who repaid her favors by preserving her beauty, the countenance of St-Tropez begged to be captured. Inside the town's Musée de l' Annonciade, painters paid tribute. Works of Paul Signac, said to have led the artists' discovery of St-Tropez, were included in the museum's first collection. Signac, a Parisian, had abandoned the short brushstrokes of impressionism

183

popular in the late 19th century to experiment with pointillism, scientifically juxtaposed dots of color. This process allowed him to capture glittering natural sunlight and, in the collections' *L'Orage*, the luminescent quality of the Golfe St-Tropez.

Charles Camoin, following Signac to St-Tropez, was a member of the *fauves*, French for "wild beasts," a derogatory term that characterized the movement's bold style. Short-lived but nevertheless significant, this process evolved from pointillism and became the bridge to modern expressionism. In "Open Window on the Harbor at St-Tropez," one of the Annonciade's best recognized paintings, Camoin departed from the wild style of the *fauves* and captured an idyllic vista of St-Tropez' port with his peaceful use of color.

Today, that same view, through a window of the Musée, looks out upon artists on the quai Jean-Jaurès, artists who stand amongst their canvasses which capture the beauty that is St-Tropez. The milieu made it easy. The buildings, the colors, the people, the sea. A bad painting difficult; a great painting probable.

———————⟶

At the villa, the day, as many before it, had flowed seamlessly. From the dining room, I gazed out over the lawn to the pool where Ira sat in the sun and read. It was three o'clock in the afternoon and this is what we did. But I had finished my novel and moved indoors. The patio table was still set with Madame's small Provençal pitcher into which I had placed wildflowers that grew around La Chandelle—my contribution to the culinary artistry of Ira's lunch.

I walked out onto the patio and sat, facing my wildflowers, Ira, the pool, the sea. The sun, which moved from east to west in an arc overhead, coordinated its hue with the golden pitcher adorned with deep-black olives. In the serenity of these afternoons, Ira and I, although aware of the other's presence, tended to our reading, our thoughts. I stood and walked to the desk where I had stored paper and a small watercolor set. While I had not exactly hidden them from Ira, I also did not call them to his attention. With a mixture of anticipation and doubt, I simply wanted to see what would happen—absent his well-intentioned encouragement.

Throughout history, all that was around had inspired this area's guests; and all that was around rewarded when captured with canvas, camera, pen. That success had emboldened intrepid experimenters—and I was about to give myself permission.

"No. I mean it. That's really good," Ira said, peering over my shoulder.

I didn't know if I could trust him. But he still made me feel special. He had walked up just as I was completing my first watercolor. I was thinking the pitcher was not symmetrical, the perspective flat. The work of a child perhaps.

But I was proud of it. Quietly proud. Proud of the product, and proud that I had ventured to do it. Happy that the long, untroubled days had provided the setting for my private adventure. I was now ready. Ready to return to the Café des Arts where I would sit among *artistes* and the spirits of those who had come before them.

I had painted a pot of flowers.

The Apprentice

INVARIABLY, SOME ESSENTIAL SYSTEM of La Chandelle will fail during our stay. The hot water heater has the disposition of a French baggage handler and will periodically go on strike. The refrigerator will develop an internal leak and short out all of the villa's electricity. The pool's filtering system will malfunction, and the aquamarine water will turn lime-green, like our Peugeot.

Knowing that Monsieur Martignon is the epitome of frugality, I try to familiarize myself with the system in question and the scope of the problem before contacting him. Our telephone ritual before he agrees to call a repairman goes something like this:

"Monsieur Martignon, how are you?"

"Very fine Monsieur Spector. I trust you and your wife are both having *de bonnes vacances?*"

"Yes, thank you. The weather has been wonderful. Yesterday we went to *la plage. La mer* was calm and warm. We had perfect swimming weather. It is a good thing, too, since *le chauffage* has broken down again and we have no hot water. We must bathe in the sea or in the pool, and it is not possible to wash the dishes or do the laundry."

"It must be inconvenient," Monsieur Martignon replies. His tone is sympathetic.

"Will you call a repairman?" I ask hopefully.

"Of course. But first may I ask you to try something? *Le chauffage* is temperamental, like my wife."

Monsieur Martignon sends me trotting off to the utility room in a far corner of La Chandelle. Inside stands a huge orange monolith featuring an unfathomable array of dials, valves, pumps, conduits, and switches. The monolith not only provides hot tap water, but heats the rooms through pipes under the floor tiles, and furnishes hot water for the pool through a heat pump. Taking it all in, I'm reminded of the engine room of the Titanic.

As instructed, I check the circuit breakers, the pilot light, the switch settings, the pressure levels, and the temperature dials. I feel which pipes are hot and which are cold. Back in the living room I pick up the phone and report my findings.

Silence. Monsieur Montignon is thinking. As a last resort, he asks me to return to the monolith and rotate the thermostat to its maximum setting. Then I'm off to the kitchen to run the hot water while counting to one hundred. Actually, I have already done these things before calling him, but I do them all again because this is our ritual.

A heavy sigh on the other end of the phone is my signal that Monsieur Martignon has capitulated. "All right," he says, "I will call my *chauffage* man. I hope he can come soon. Please give my regards to Madame Spector. *Au revoir.*"

As a result of the occasional malfunction, I have greeted a variety of French repairmen at our villa. They are easily distinguished from their American counterparts by an unusually high degree of specialization. The domain of the water heater repairman, for example, does not extend beyond the heater's physical dimensions. The gas, electric, and water lines connected to it are the sole purview of the gasman, the electrician, and the plumber, respectively.

I shudder to think what would happen if *le chauffage* ever suffered a compound problem. I imagined an army of specialists, all five foot seven inches tall, standing around the monolith while they boisterously negotiated a treaty that divided up the territory of the water heater as if it were post-war Germany.

French repairmen are also distinguished by their adherence to the apprentice system. In fact, the apprentice, a young man in his twenties, always made the initial service call. I assumed this was Monsieur Martignon's doing. I assumed he had told the repair shop that there were Americans inhabiting the villa, and therefore the failure must be obvious. Evidently, his renters had neglected to observe a simple warning label and a circuit breaker had blown. In other words, he had instructed the shop to send the apprentice, the person who billed at the lowest labor rate.

The day after advising Monsieur of our situation with *le chauffage*, the apprentice, a young man in coveralls, arrived at the front gate. We exchanged pleasantries in French and, as with other apprentices I've met, he professed not to know a word of English.

I was eager for him to attack our problem, but before that could happen, custom must be followed. This meant escorting the young man into the kitchen and offering him *quelque chose à boire*—something to drink. Over time, I have learned that Orangina is the French repairman's beverage of choice.

While he sipped his drink, the apprentice turned on the faucet and held his free hand under the hot water tap. After a moment of contemplation he announced, *"Pas chaud."*

"Oui, pas chaud," I repeated, feeling relieved that at least the right specialist was on the case. After refilling his glass, it was time to move on to the utility room. As he stood looking up at the monolith—and

despite my protestations that I didn't comprehend anything he said—he began a lengthy soliloquy in French techno-speak. To me it sounded as if he were reciting everything he had learned in *chauffage* school.

Although the apprentice spent an hour removing panels, fiddling with knobs, turning valves, and drinking Orangina, the monolith, which roars like a lion when functioning properly, remained as quiescent as a kitten napping through a cold winter's afternoon. But just to be on the safe side, the two of us returned to the kitchen. While I topped off his glass with Orangina, the apprentice ran the hot water again, thoughtfully sipped his drink, and shook his head gravely. *"Toujours pas chaud."*

I shook my head gravely as well. *"Toujours pas chaud,"* I repeated. It was an opportunity for us to bond.

A flurry of gestures followed, and I gathered the problem with *le chauffage* was *"trés mal,"* and that a second and more intensive repair effort would occur the next day.

When the apprentice departed, I broke the news to Barbara. Needless to say, she wasn't happy about having to bathe in the pool again. After two days, we were "itching" to take a regular bath, but we didn't want to compound our repair problem by using soap and shampoo, and risk upsetting *la piscine's* delicate pH balance. I pictured the filtering system churning the contaminated water, the surface foaming, and lime-green bubbles slowly rising into the blue sky.

The next day an older man in coveralls appeared at the gate. He spoke English perfectly and I learned that he owned the repair shop. Following the pleasantries and the Orangina, he entered the utility room, flipped a switch on the monolith, removed a rear panel, and wrapped a valve sharply with a ball peen hammer. The pilot light ignited, and the water heater roared to life. He replaced the panel, shook my hand, and wished me a good day as he padded down the driveway. I had the feeling he had been here before. I also had the feeling that master repairmen did not coddle their apprentices by sharing maintenance tips, or by supplying them with ball peen hammers.

One season, the hammer trick didn't work and a thermocouple had to be ordered from Paris. The master repairman regrettably informed us that it would take several days before we would have hot water again.

Clearly, it was time for a meeting of the Board of Directors of La Chandelle.

"Let's shutter the villa and stay in St-Tropez until the water heater is fixed," I suggested. "As parsimonious as Monsieur Martignon is, I'm certain he won't make us pay for the days we can't stay here."

"Which hotel do you have in mind?"

"How about the Byblos?" I knew it would be pricey, but our situation required drastic action.

Barbara perked up. "The Byblos sounds great . . . but we desperately need to do our laundry—there's no way I'm entering their elegant lobby without changing into clean clothes."

We decided to go to the tourist bureau and inquire about coin-operated laundries. The clerk was helpful. She told us that every major town had at least one Laundromat. She recommended the "Hollywood Lavarie" in the town of St-Aygulf, about fifteen minutes away. She said it was more of a working town than St-Tropez or Ste-Maxime, so if we went during the workday, we wouldn't have to fight for access to a machine.

We loaded the Peugeot with dirty laundry and locked up the villa. The address took us to a sleepy side street near St-Aygulf's beachfront. With each of us carrying an armful of dirty clothing, we entered an empty room lined with washers and dryers. Vintage movie posters covered the walls, mostly portraying B films and actors from the middle of the last century. One poster featured a young Ronald Reagan addressing labels attached to cigarette cartons. A green and red wreath on the wall placed the time at Christmas. The tagline said, "I'm sending Chesterfields to all my friends. That's the merriest Christmas any smoker can have."

I felt a shoulder nudge me. "Let's get on with it," Barbara said, peering over her armload of laundry.

I returned to the washing machines. I knew from *le chauffage* that the French had their own peculiar way of designing appliances, so it wasn't surprising that I had no clue as to how any of the machines operated. Fortunately, there were detailed instructions in English. In fact, with the exception of the washers and dryers themselves, everything about the Laundromat—the name, the movie posters, the Coke machine, the instructions—seemed calculated to attract Americans.

I turned back to Barbara. "Don't you think it's ironic that we have French laundries in America while they have American laundries in France?"

"No I don't. Let's just get on with it—okay?"

The instructions explained that everything—the bleach and soap dispensing machines, the washer and dryer capacity, the program selection—were all dictated by the wash load in kilograms. The load size, in turn, dictated the number of coins. With a single load costing as much as fifteen euros, the owner of the Hollywood Lavarie must believe that Americans treat European coins like Monopoly money. We could only guess at the number of kilograms we had, but one thing was certain: the machines' appetite for *pièces de monnaie* seemed insatiable.

When our laundry had made it safely out of the dryer, we walked down to the beach with a couple of towels and the outfits we had chosen for the Byblos. Changing on the beach is a national pastime in France, and having observed women pull bras through their sleeves and men wrap towels around their waists to replace wet swimsuits with dry shorts, we adroitly put on our freshly laundered clothes.

After three days at the beautiful Byblos, we came back to an abundance of hot water and an apologetic note from Monsieur Martignon, including an adjustment to our rent. I shuddered to think what our opinion of villa life would have been if we had only booked one week, and had to face several days with a broken-down water heater. But a month gave us time in abundance and, as Barbara and I dined on the patio, we reflected how the *chauffage* incident was more of an adventure than an inconvenience, and how easy it was to fall back into the unhurried rhythm that was La Chandelle.

The Beautiful People

WE ARE ADDICTED to St-Tropez, driven to it like a Frenchman to his paramour. We never tire of sitting at the outdoor cafés, sipping wine, watching the beautiful people promenade along the quai Jean-Jaurès like models on a runway, giving us a preview of the styles that will be *en vogue* in America next year. We never tire of wandering through the maze of cobblestone backstreets, through the living museum of alleys and archways that are unchanged even after hundreds of years. And we never tire of watching the portraitists along the harbor as they capture their subjects in shades of soft pencil.

That's where we met Laszlo.

We were looking for someone to draw Maggie, our neighbor's angelic five-year-old girl. We had a snapshot of the child, and the plan was to surprise our neighbors with a life-sized rendering in appreciation for watching our house while we were away.

We found the portraitist sitting idly under an umbrella, seemingly indifferent to the multimillion-dollar yachts at his back, and to the human spectacle passing before him. He was showcasing drawings of angelic children, so Barbara and I stepped out of the parade for a closer look.

The artist smiled. "You like my portraits?" he asked, somehow divining we spoke English.

"Yes," I said. "Can you work from this photograph?" I handed him the snapshot.

"Elle est un bel enfant," he remarked as he studied the picture. "Sure, I can do it."

195

"How much?" I inquired.

"It is 150 euros to work from a photograph. But your beautiful child is worth it, yes?"

"Actually, she's our neighbor's child. The portrait's a gift and I'm afraid we can't pay more than 100 euros." It looked as if the fellow had been idle for a while, so I figured it was a buyer's market. "But there's no rush," I added. "I'll leave the photograph so you can draw the little girl when you have the time."

"Sure. I will do it for you for 100 euros. It will be ready on Wednesday," he said, disarming us with a broad smile.

We exchanged names and said goodbye. His was Laszlo, and Barbara and I felt fortunate to have found a charming gentleman who spoke English and specialized in drawing angelic children. We would soon learn that Laszlo was indeed a man of many talents, but portrait art was not among them.

The following Wednesday we found Lazlo at his station. He chatted with us amiably as he carefully withdrew Maggie's drawing from a brown paper sheath. We were hoping he had captured the rays of Irish sunshine in her face, but we would happily accept any reasonable interpretation, from Norman Rockwell to Margaret Keane.

We received, instead, the face of Linda Blair in "The Exorcist," just after her head had rotated 360 degrees.

Laszlo smiled proudly as he held the portrait up. "Good, yes?" he said.

"Ah . . . ah," I stammered, reflexively backing away and bumping into Barbara, who had been staring at the drawing in wide-eyed disbelief.

"Good, yes?" Laszlo repeated, grinning broadly.

"I'm afraid it doesn't *quite* capture the little girl," I said when I finally managed to speak. "For one thing, Maggie doesn't have dark circles under her eyes. And for another, her incisors aren't razor-sharp."

The artist continued to smile. "No problem," he said, removing an eraser from his easel. "I can fix."

Laszlo began working on the portrait as my wife and I conferred a few steps away.

"He's turned Maggie into a monster!" Barbara said none too softly. "We can't give that *thing* to our neighbors! What are we supposed to say, 'Thanks for watching our house and this is what we *really* think of your little girl?'" Barbara's voice was rising by the second.

"S-h-h-h," I said, glancing at Laszlo who was hunched over his easel, seemingly oblivious to us. "Maybe he *can* fix."

Barbara shook her head. "Give me a break. There's *no* way any eraser is going to turn that devil into an angel! We just threw away 100 euros!"

"S-h-h-h," I repeated, touching my forefinger to my lips. But getting my wife to calm down once she gets going is akin to drinking water from a fire hose.

Suddenly Laszlo's head lifted, a hand motioned, and we gathered around his easel. "*C'est bon, oui?*" he said, trying French this time as he offered his drawing.

Barbara had been right. The changes were minimal, but at least Maggie's fangs no longer glinted in the light.

"Yes, it's better," I conceded. "But it still doesn't quite capture the little girl. Can I see the photograph?" I asked, stalling for time.

Laszlo handed me the original. "It is more difficult to make likeness from photo. Real people are easier. Yes?"

"Uh-huh," I nodded as I held the print next to the drawing. But no matter how hard I squinted, it was still Maggie in the photo and a devil-child in the portrait. I turned to Laszlo. "Is it possible for you to make the little girl's eyes larger and move them further apart? And can you remove the sneer from her lips?" I knew I was pushing Laszlo, and I was hoping eye enlargement and sneer removal wouldn't jack the price back up to 150 euros.

Laszlo's smile suddenly evaporated. *"Je ferai mon meilleur,"* he muttered. "I will do my best. You come back later." He pointed across the street. "Café de Paris is a good place to have a drink, watch people. I will wave when the portrait is ready."

This was our first hint that Laszlo knew his way around town. Of the many wonderful sidewalk cafés, we favored the Café de Paris. "Okay," I said.

"He just wants us to get plastered so we'll accept his portrait and pay him," Barbara remarked as we crossed the street.

"He's probably right."

It was still early so we had our choice of tables. We took one in the front row and ordered wine. As we sipped, we briefly entertained the idea of ducking out the back. But by the time our second glass arrived, we decided to face the situation.

Meanwhile, across the street, Laszlo remained huddled over Maggie as if trying to resuscitate her.

By our third glass, we knew we would pay the man and take the drawing no matter what. Our alternative was cutting a wide swath around the street artists every time we visited St-Tropez' port.

"And what are we going to do with the devil-child?" Barbara asked. "You're not suggesting we take it home?"

I downed my wine. "Why not? We can store it in our garage, and if our neighbors ever piss us off, we'll take it out and give it to them."

Out of the corner of my eye I saw Laszlo waving. He was ready. We gathered again in front of his easel. I took a deep breath and studied Maggie. Yes, Laszlo had made some improvements. Still, no matter how I tilted my head, the little girl's cold lethal stare held my eyes. It was as if she knew she would be coming home with us.

Looking back, paying the artist and graciously accepting his work had been the right thing to do. One hundred euros was a small sum to pay for a connection with someone who had a wealth of information about St-Tropez. Laszlo knew the best restaurants, the best jazz spots, the best tour boats, the best shops, and which of the town's events were not to be missed. Over time we became friends and stopped to chat whenever we found him at his station.

One day, we decided it was time to experience St-Tropez' legendary late-night action. But this would take special planning because we were now in a zone, gliding through life, allowing our body rhythms to guide our daily routine. In other words, we were usually asleep by midnight.

Naturally, we sought Laszlo's advice on the matter. He had customers for a change, and we watched in silent amusement as he turned three generations of a Swedish family into an excellent rendition of the Munsters. After receiving payment from his stunned subjects, he greeted us with his trademark smile.

"Can you recommend a nightclub for next Saturday?" I asked.

"Sure."

"Do you think we should go to a jazz place or to the disco?"

"The disco, definitely," Laszlo said, swaying his hips to imaginary music. *"Laissez les bon temps roulez!"*

"Which disco?"

"Les Caves du Roi at the Hôtel Byblos is best. You may see Gerard Depardieu and Catherine Deneuve. Perhaps Jean-Paul Belmondo and Yves Saint Laurent. But it is very expensive."

"How expensive?"

Laszlo waved the 200 euros he had just received from the Swedes. "This will buy a bottle of champagne, perhaps. I think the disco behind Musée de l'Annonciade is better for you."

Laszlo was probably recalling how I had haggled over the price of "Maggie the Monster-Child."

"Do you go there?" I inquired.

The artist shook his head sadly. "Not any more. The owner is angry with me."

I didn't pry. I figured the owner's daughter had once sat for Laszlo.

"But it is a good place. All my friends go."

"What time do they go?"

"One, maybe two in the morning. But it does not get crazy until three. Then *les bon temps roulent* until dawn." Laszlo swayed his hips again.

"Three o'clock in the morning?" Barbara said, looking at me. "We're in big trouble."

When Saturday evening arrived, we delayed dinner until ten, drawing out our meal until the restaurant closed at midnight. Then we spent another hour in a holding pattern at the Hôtel Sube's bar, first sipping a potent Provençal *eau de vie* called marc, then shifting to cappuccinos to stay conscious.

Nearby, several small tables had been moved together, allowing four chic Tropeziénne couples to sit in intimate proximity. The men had short and stylish hair, and wore tight designer pants and knit shirts; the women were tanned, beautiful, and adorned with clinging swatches of material that left little to the imagination. And like the young locals we had seen at the Hôtel Sube's bar before, they were ignoring their drinks in favor of each other.

It was easy to see why.

These were *les belles personnes* of St-Tropez, the arbiters of beauty and fashion, members of the inside group that promenaded in front of the sidewalk cafés while the rest of us stared at them. As they laughed and touched, the room seemed to fill with sensuality.

The bell in the church steeple rang once to signal 1:00 a.m., the official hour of *les bon temps*. Barbara and I slogged out of the hotel behind the beautiful people. We weren't sure where the group was going until they turned into a small plaza behind the Musée de l'Annonciade and entered the disco. Along the way they continued to laugh and touch, in anticipation, I imagined, of smoothly sliding from their amorous bar scene into an evening of sexually charged dancing. Barbara and I, on the other hand, were at risk of smoothly sliding into sleep.

We plopped into a padded booth across the dance floor from *les belles personnes,* and then watched more of the same filter in as colored lights flashed and pulsated to the mechanized thumping of French disco music. But in Tropeziénne time, the evening was still young, and at this juncture, only the ceiling strobes were dancing on the floor.

A tuxedoed waiter approached. We ordered a bottle of *l'eau gazeuse*—plain sparkling water. He politely informed us that it would cost 100 euros, the same as a bottle of wine, a bottle of champagne, or one of Laszlo's bargain portraits.

After the waiter left, I let the pull of gravity, the pulsating music, and the strobes drive me into the banquette. More people drifted in, but the floor remained empty.

"Wanna take a spin?" I finally said. Barbara had been sinking as well, and only her head remained visible above the table. I figured I had to get her moving before she disappeared altogether.

"Ha," she answered weakly.

Our precious sparkling water arrived and we sipped it slowly, savoring it like a rare wine. The minutes dragged on, the dance floor remained empty, and I was using my thumb and forefinger to hold one of my eyelids open. I knew I was in big trouble when the thumping music began to sound like a distant, syncopated lullaby.

I was about to throw in the towel and suggest we crawl home when, suddenly, the women from the Hôtel Sube took to the floor and began dancing in a circle. After a few minutes, the men got up and surrounded their dates like Indians around a wagon train. But the women tightened the circle and refused to yield anything but their bare backs, a ritual that continued until the song ended and the dancers returned to their seats.

This bizarre behavior left us with questions: Why were the women rebuffing the advances of their boyfriends? Did they think dancing with males was *passé* in the disco? We didn't have a clue.

But one thing was clear: all of *les belles personnes* were unable to dance. They shuffled their feet and shifted their weight, they swayed their shoulders and waved their arms, but at no time were they ever in sync with the music.

"*Les belles personnes* are about as funky as Japanese Sumo wrestlers," I said.

The song changed and Barbara suddenly came alive. "It's 'Dancing Queen.' I love that song," she said, sitting up and moving her shoulders to the beat.

"Let's show them how it's *really* done," I said, suddenly feeling energized as well. We are decent disco dancers, and once even won a contest.

"Yes, let's," Barbara said, taking my hand.

As we moved to the middle of the dance floor, the DJ must have sensed our intentions because "Dancing Queen" segued into "Disco Inferno." Conversations ceased and all eyes were upon us as we performed our "Saturday Night Fever" routine.

For that brief moment in time, *we* were in our element; *we* were the beautiful people of St-Tropez.

Ecstasy at Your Feet

E VERY SEASON, Monsieur Montignon remained perplexed by our resistance to his touring suggestions. He seemed to have an endless list of twelfth-century charterhouses he wanted us to experience, all of which were "surrounded by forested beauty and readily accessible by mountain goat trails that ran perilously close to the edge of sheer cliffs." In truth, those last words were not his; it was only my imagination at work after the Chartreuse de La Verne incident.

"We actually *do* leave the villa—we really do," I told Monsieur Montignon during one of our telephone exchanges. I explained that we had visited the Picasso Museum in Antibes and the Matisse Museum in Nice, among other tourist attractions along the Côte d'Azur.

I heard Monsieur Martignon sigh on the other end of the line. "But Monsieur Spector, it is not the same thing. You will only find *la belle Provence* inland, in the small villages, the hilltop towns, and in the beauty of the forests and the mountains."

"*Peut-être demain*—maybe tomorrow," I said.

⟶

I now found irony in my predisposition to cling to the villa. Reaching back to those days before our first season in the South of France, I had wondered what it would be like to have nothing to do and an entire month in which to do it. I wondered if Barbara's "Enchanted April" experiment would send me screaming from the villa. For insurance, I worked hard to convince my wife that we should take a trip, a mid-month break from villa life just in case her month of unplanned and uninterrupted time needed fine tuning. "We could stay at some hot European destination," I suggested, "and use the opportunity to review our vacation. Then we could make any necessary adjustments to ensure that the remainder of the month ran—"

"—in other words," Barbara interrupted, "you're deathly afraid of becoming bored."

My wife was right, of course, and she continued objecting to the idea of taking a mid-month break until I showed her a color brochure describing the Villa d'Este on Lake Como.

"Check this out," I said. "Can't you just picture us strolling arm-in-arm through these beautiful grounds while small wooden boats glide idly on the lake? It'll be like living in a Merchant Ivory movie. I'll wear a white linen suit."

Barbara glanced casually at the brochure.

"Look at that swimming pool," I said. "It's actually floating on the lake. And notice the *trompe l'oeil* façades, and the portico and its colonnades."

"Yes, it's all very beautiful. And which future vacation would this be for?"

"The hotel is only a day's travel from the Var. We can take the Côte d'Azur train. It follows the Mediterranean coastline all the way into Italy. It's one of the most scenic train rides in the world. On one side of the tracks is the sea; on the other the Esterel mountains. We switch trains in Italy for another scenic ride north into the lake region."

Barbara cupped her ear. "I'm sorry, I must have missed *which* future vacation you said this would be for."

I sighed. "Okay, this vacation. We can go in the middle of June."

Barbara relented only because the Villa d'Este was one of the resorts she had always wanted to visit. But as my penance for nudging her, it fell upon me to make the arrangements.

Unfortunately, the hotel was fully booked and there were no rooms available. We were put on a waiting list, with the only consolation being that the reservationist, a classy gentleman who spoke English with a sonorous Italian accent, said he would note that our arrival date was flexible and that we could travel to Lake Como from the Côte d'Azur on short notice.

———

Two weeks into our stay at La Chandelle, I had completely forgotten about the Villa d'Este. We were comfortably ensconced, and Barbara and I were enjoying ourselves much more than either of us had anticipated. It was difficult to imagine being anywhere else.

Early one afternoon, as we were preparing to have lunch, we received a telephone call that complicated our lives. The Villa d'Este informed us that a lake view room had just become available for three nights beginning the day after tomorrow. The hotel requested an answer within the hour as the waiting list for this particular room was quite long.

I found Barbara setting the table in the shade of one of our *parasol pine* trees. Down the hill, bright white sailboats crisscrossed a sapphire sea. "What do you think about leaving here for a few days in Italy?" I asked, taking a seat.

My wife's stress-free face suddenly showed a hint of tension.

"On the one hand," I said, "I'd love to stay at the Villa d'Este. We may never have a better opportunity. But on the other hand, we'll have to pack, stow the outdoor furniture, close up the villa, and then travel by train all day and into the night. Then we'll have to reverse the process three days later.

"That telephone call caught me off guard, and traveling into Italy now feels somewhat burdensome. Besides, my butt seems stuck to this chair."

"It isn't an easy decision," Barbara agreed. "As much as I want to experience the Villa d'Este, I don't want to lose the wonderful rhythm we've established here."

So we ended up passing on the palatial Villa d'Este in favor of our modest country home. "Enchanted April," we knew, would now play to the end without intermission.

⌁

In January of the following year, with five months to go before we would return to the South of France, our life at La Chandelle seemed faraway, dreamlike, surreal. Even Barbara wondered if the extraordinary peace and tranquility we had felt would continue, or would the novelty of a month-long vacation at the villa wear off?

As a hedge, we made a list of daytrips we could take should the spirit move us. High on our list were Port Grimaud, the Venice of Southern France; the old quarter of Nice; the beach at Cannes; and the picturesque, deep harbor port of Villefranche. And learning from the Villa d'Este episode, we planned a more realistic two-day stay at the Hôtel du Cap-Eden Roc in Antibes—the most exclusive hotel on the Côte d'Azur and an easy hour's drive from Ste-Maxime.

If any resort could test the magic spell of La Chandelle, it would be the "Cap"—as it is affectionately known to insiders. The resort was situated at the tip of a peninsula between Cannes and Nice. F. Scott Fitzgerald modeled the Hôtel des Étrangers after the Cap in *Tender is the Night.* And in "Truth or Dare," Madonna grabbed her various body parts while dancers gyrated behind her under the fountains. Antonio Banderas, Cher, Robert Redford, Holly Hunter, Sean Connery, Tom Cruise, and Cindy Crawford were among the celebrities who had vacationed there.

By booking months in advance, we secured two nights in the third week of June. The tariff was steep, but we rationalized it as a chance to pretend we were high-rolling members of the Lost Generation. I pictured us at the terrace bar. The sun would be setting while a sea breeze chased away the warm afternoon air. I imagined myself dressed in that white linen suit I had planned for the Villa d'Este as we waited for our perfectly chilled martinis to arrive.

This time it would be easier to leave La Chandelle.

Or so we thought.

On the eve of the last day to cancel the Cap without losing our hefty deposit, we were dining at the villa, enjoying a particularly spectacular meal on the patio. The air was soft and the last rays of the sun had turned the stucco homes on the hills into bars of gold. We were mid-meal, eating a tangy sorbet I had made by blending Campari, orange juice, lemon, and sugar. It matched the color of the sky. La Chandelle was conspiring with the air, the light, the food, and the wine to seduce us once again.

And if that weren't enough, Barbara chose this night to introduce something new to our dining experience.

"Call it the 'performance intermezzo,'" she said. "Between courses we'll share a passage from our journals, or something from a book we're reading, or a drawing, or a poem—anything at all. I'll go first. I'll read something from Franz Kafka that seems appropriate at the moment:

> *Remain sitting at your table and listen.*
> *Do not even listen, simply wait, be quiet,*
> *still, and solitary. The world will freely offer*
> *itself to you to be unmasked; it has no choice,*
> *it will roll in ecstasy at your feet."*

There was silence for a long time. Finally, I said. "What are the odds?"

Barbara knew exactly what I was talking about. "I'd say fifty-fifty. And you?"

"About the same."

"We have until tomorrow to cancel the Cap. How do we decide?" she asked.

The last thing I wanted added to a memorable meal was a healthy serving of indecision. "I have an idea. As *my* performance intermezzo, I'll read to you about the hotel. The information we brought from home contains plenty of superlatives. Perhaps we just need to remind ourselves why we were so anxious to stay there in the first place. After I'm finished, we'll take a vote of the Board of Directors."

"And if we're deadlocked?"

"We'll flip a franc."

"Deal."

After the main course, a fabulous *rôti d'agneau*, I returned to the table with a file folder. Barbara stood behind me and placed her hands on my shoulders as I began reading from a magazine clipping: "No hotel in the Riviera has a better approach to the sea. Limestone steps take guests to a spectacular tree-lined *allée* that leads down to the Mediterranean."

"Go on."

"Both the restaurant, multi-tiered like a cruise ship and cantilevered over the sea, and the pool, carved out of the cliff face, offer incredible views of the Mediterranean Sea and the Îles de Lérins in the distance."

"Sounds wonderful."

I scanned the article for more of the same. "Wait a second . . . here's something I hadn't noticed before."

"Yes?"

"It's a discussion about the celebrity guests: 'If you're a Somebody, the service is exemplary. But if you're a Nobody, you get that level of service only if you tip accordingly.'"

"Does the article mention what kind of tips we are talking about?"

I continued reading. "If the bellhop brings a bucket of ice to the room, we're supposed to tip 10 euros. If we have something dry-cleaned, a 50-euro tip is expected."

I paused while Barbara mentally performed the conversion. "Fifty dollars to deliver dry cleaning?"

"That gives me second thoughts about wearing a white linen suit," I said. "But compared to the cost of the room and the meals, these exorbitant tips don't bother me as much as having to figure out the rules— what is appropriate and when. It doesn't sound peaceful."

"I agree," Barbara said.

I closed the folder. "Shall I assume we can waive the formal vote?"

"Yes."

And so we decided to pass on the stellar Cap. Barbara put her arms around me. "I want to share something with you. As the days go by, I keep thinking our life in this place can't get any better. But it always does. For example, your dinner tonight was the best."

I turned my head sideways and smiled. "You said the same thing last night."

"And that is precisely the point, isn't it, Monsieur?"

"Yes, and shall I also assume the service was exquisite, Madame?"

"Absolutely, Monsieur."

"And what exorbitant tip will you give *me*?"

"Some advice." Barbara leaned toward my ear. *"Le bonheur est ici*—happiness is here."

Farniente

ONE DAY IT ALL came together. It happened as we floated on our rafts in the pool; when the sun lingered at its zenith and the sea mirrored the deep blue sky; when the temperature of the water and the air were both a balmy seventy-eight degrees, and it was hard to tell where one ended and the other began. As my raft neared Barbara's, I took her hand and we began to rotate together, in the gentle vortex of the pool's circulating waters.

"The French have a special word for this moment," she said. *"Farniente."*

I turned my head toward her. "Doing nothing?"

"It means more than that. In context it refers to a state of deep relaxation, free of stress, free of day-to-day concerns. French resorts promise *farniente*, and show serene-looking guests lying in the sun with their eyes closed."

"Like the way the French behave at the beach?"

"Exactly."

"I've noticed that once settled in, they don't move except to turn over. Even the Italians, who are often quite lively, become unusually quiet at the beach."

"The Italians also practice *farniente*. Only they call it *dolce far niente* or 'sweet idleness.'"

Farniente. The word was perfect. Now I understood why our ambitions to tour villages, visit museums, or spend the day exploring the countryside receded as the sun climbed in the sky, and the diamond-studded waters of the infinity pool or the Mediterranean beckoned. Now I understood why I had difficulty describing villa life to friends back home. There was no equivalent term in English, and the best I was able to do was dredge up clichéd words like "peaceful" and "tranquil," which made it sound as if we had spent the month as patients at a sanitarium. But now, backed by an official European cultural phenomenon, I could say with confidence that we practiced *farniente,* and at a minimum our friends would think we were doing something special because there was a French word involved.

Floating on my raft, still turning, I idly watched an overhanging *pin parasol* branch rotate above me. I was thinking about a dinner conversation that took place shortly after Barbara and I returned from our first season. A friend had asked me to explain the difference between renting a villa and staying at a hotel. "There's no comparison," I replied with an almost religious fervor. "Although hotels try to make you feel comfortable, some level of intrusion is always present. There's the chambermaid in the morning, the mini bar guy in the afternoon and, in between, the noises of strangers living around you. There's a timetable for meals, and an implied code of dress and behavior.

"But at the villa, there were no intrusions, no deadlines, no strangers. Barbara and I achieved a level of peace not possible at a hotel."

Lacking the term *farniente* at the time, I went on to describe how we were perfectly happy to remain at the pool although there were numerous sights to see all around us, and how even hanging the laundry and mowing the lawn were enjoyable.

Our friend, a busy professional predisposed to relentless touring while on vacation, received my homily with glazed-over eyes. This was my cue that I needed to present a more balanced picture. "Admittedly, there were a few obstacles to overcome," I added.

"Such as?"

"Well, at the beginning of our season, we had to drive to the villa through a monsoon on a high-speed toll road. In spite of flooding, zero visibility, and a huge, multi-vehicle wreck, the French drove through the deluge with their accelerators pressed to the floor. Barbara and I were terrified. Then we became trapped in an automated tollbooth because I didn't have any coins. When we finally arrived at the villa, the key wasn't hidden where it was supposed to be so we were locked out for several hours until the landlord showed up."

"Uh-huh."

"Then, after settling in, we had the mistral, a huge windstorm that swooped down the mountains and blew copious amounts of organic debris into the pool, turning it into pea soup. The prescribed remedy, according to the landlord, was to add salt, stir, and taste. Then the villa's water heater broke down, and when hitting it with a hammer didn't work, we went to a hotel to clean up."

"Sounds like great fun."

"There were also a few obstacles to overcome when we did venture into the countryside because we were unfamiliar with French infrastructure. But once we learned how to extricate ourselves from the parking lots, how to careen through the traffic circles, and how to avoid narrow, mountain roads with no guard rails and sheer vertical drops, things went much more smoothly."

"I'll bet."

"Well, you had to be there," I said, changing the subject before my friend had the chance.

Although floating on our rafts was a perfect metaphor for the timeless, seamless circularity of our days at the villa, we knew *farniente* was too good a term to limit to lounging about the pool. Over time it came to mean dining on the patio, watching the sky turn red and the *petits bateaux* sailing back to port; it came to mean leisurely after-dinner strolls around the neighborhood; it came to mean jogging in the hills, climbing higher and higher until we were rewarded by the meandering coastline of an azure Mediterranean sea; it came to mean dining at a restaurant in St-Tropez and foregoing dessert in favor of a *petite glace* at the marina, savoring the rich ice cream as a fascinating mix of stylish locals and kitschy tourists paraded in front of us.

Our *farniente*-filled days flowed one into the next until we began to notice that the cooing of the doves and the chirping of the cicadas were now being interrupted by accordion music, singing, and bursts of laughter. The villas around us were coming alive as European city dwellers claimed their parcels of French paradise. It was the end of June, and as our season drew to a close, Barbara and I wondered if we would be able to take *farniente* back to America. We wondered how it could survive in the real world of commuter traffic, of bills and voicemails, of sensory overload. How could we spare the time for long lunches, naps in the afternoon, and elaborate dinners in the evening?

The answer, we concluded, lay in the very concept that brought us to the South of France in the first place.

We would give ourselves permission.

We would arrest busy moments, empty them of future deadlines and obligations, and fill them with the present—we might draw, write, think, read, or simply enjoy each other's company. While we knew it would be impractical to duplicate La Chandelle, villa life had given us an extraordinary insight about *farniente*, an insight we would nurture until it was June again, and time to return home.

Le Pied

"Why do the French say le pied to describe something really great? It makes no sense—pied means feet."

"They are referring to the curling of a person's toes during sex."

"Oh."

HOW CAN YOU justify an entire month of unplanned time only to learn that all you deem important may not be indispensable? That you may not be indispensable?

Rather—how can you not.

How can you not allow yourself to feel the freedom that you have denied yourself for years? For decades? For your entire life? How do you accept changing the patterns that have always defined you?

By the strength gained in giving yourself the permission to do nothing—enabling you to look at all you have ever considered important from a new perspective. By no longer being bound to a perceived reality that may not have existed. By freedom from those restraints that limited what you did or how you did it, allowing you to do things differently, better. It can build upon itself, freedom becoming power, all becoming increased happiness.

And it can happen from the joy of a green pool made blue again by a salt infusion, stirred by a Bunyonesque-sized wooden spoon. By a rollerblading clerk saving you from French humiliation. By escaping a human-ingesting *pissoir* to see the light.

It may happen in the South of France. Or at a nearby lake. Or in a mountain cabin. It begins without, and moves within. Then it all seems so simple. And that is the point. When you do it, it all seems so simple—and so right.

Unstructured and uninterrupted time. Its experience lives on.

Le Pied.

~*Barbara Spector*

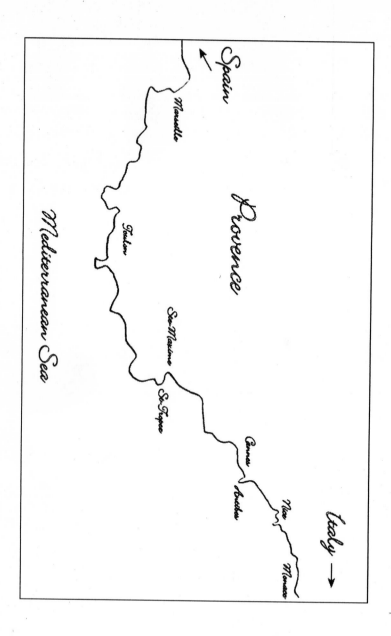

Spain

Provence

Marseille

Toulon

St-Maxime

St-Tropez

Cannes

Antibes

Nice

Monaco

Italy →

Mediterranean Sea